MW01489591

Overthinking Detox

7 Practical Strategies to Reduce Stress,
Clear Your Mind, and Live
in the Present

Russell Di

© Copyright 2024 - All rights reserved.

The content contained within this book may not be reproduced, duplicated or transmitted without direct written permission from the author or the publisher.

Under no circumstances will any blame or legal responsibility be held against the publisher, or author, for any damages, reparation, or monetary loss due to the information contained within this book, either directly or indirectly.

Legal Notice:

This book is copyright protected. It is only for personal use. You cannot amend, distribute, sell, use, quote or paraphrase any part, or the content within this book, without the consent of the author or publisher.

Disclaimer Notice:

Please note the information contained within this document is for educational and entertainment purposes only. All effort has been executed to present accurate, up to date, reliable, complete information. No warranties of any kind are declared or implied. Readers acknowledge that the author is not engaged in the rendering of legal, financial, medical or professional advice. The content within this book has been derived from various sources. Please consult a licensed professional before attempting any techniques outlined in this book.

By reading this document, the reader agrees that under no circumstances is the author responsible for any losses, direct or indirect, that are incurred as a result of the use of the information contained within this document, including, but not limited to, errors, omissions, or inaccuracies.

Table of Contents

Introduction:

In Need of a Mind Cleanse

I couldn't sleep. I had not been able to get a proper night's rest for a while, and I didn't know why. I was doing great on my exams, everything was fine at home, and I had just met a nice girl. Still, as soon as I turned off the lights, everything started moving around—and I mean, in my head. I was overwhelmed with thoughts, and they kept me up for several hours until I finally dozed off.

Although I had slowly gotten used to waking up grumpy and with a stiff neck, I refused to address the issue. "There is nothing wrong with me. I have no major problems. It's just my overthinking." But guess what? Overthinking *is* a problem in itself!

Do you know how uncomfortable you feel when you enter a room that is all cluttered, filled with half-empty boxes, papers scattered on the floor, and dirty clothes lying around? That is what your mind feels when you are overthinking. It doesn't matter if the walls are solid and the ceiling has a new layer of spotless paint: Being in that room still feels *wrong*. Fortunately, it is easier to pick up dirty clothes, get rid of the boxes, put things back into place, and clean up than to mend a hole in the ceiling.

We all overthink from time to time, but if you are struggling with overthinking—or "mental clutter" to the point that it affects your daily life, then it is time for a cleanup!

What Is Normal and What Is Not When It Comes to Overthinking?

Imagine you have been offered a job abroad, but your partner can't join you because they have to look after a sick parent. Or that you have a huge exam in the morning, and although you have studied, you keep thinking about the questions they may ask you and wondering how you will do in front of the intimidating examination table.

We all overthink at some point in our lives. Some big decisions require a lot of mental energy. However, for some people, overthinking becomes a daily habit that gets in the way of decision-making and relationships and also takes a toll on their health. How can you tell if overthinking is a problem for you? Well, I don't believe you have picked this book if it weren't, for a start! After all, you don't consider a whole house cleanup for a single cluttered drawer or a few dirty plates in the sink.

If you are struggling with overthinking regularly, these are some ways it may affect you:

- You struggle with any decision, not only the big ones.

- After the slightest argument with your partner, a friend, or someone from work, you find yourself going over the conversation until it has started to affect your relationships.

- Your perfectionism makes you unable to finish tasks in time because you feel they are not *quite* right.

- You lie awake imagining catastrophic scenarios that will most likely never occur.

- You keep imagining "What ifs" and regretting what could have been.

- You may feel isolated but still keep avoiding social situations.

Despite what you may have heard—maybe from well-intentioned friends or relatives—no, overthinking is *not* all in your head. Although it is not classified as a mental illness (Nelson, 2023), it can take a toll on your health. According to science, overthinking can contribute to developing health problems such as high blood pressure, sleep problems, appetite suppression and digestive issues, headaches, and a weakened immune system (Gupta, 2022). Additionally, it serves as a risk factor for mental health conditions such as depression and anxiety.

Again, overthinking is not a disease. But just like a cluttered house accumulates dirt and can attract pests, all that mental clutter you carry ends up hurting you.

How the Right Strategies Will Improve Your Life

I have always lived in big cities, and I believe their loud and fast environment contributes to my passion for understanding the complexities of human behavior and my overthinking tendencies. However, mental clutter is no longer an interference in my life. Over the years, I have developed a tool kit by combining healthy habits, mindfulness, and cognitive behavioral strategies to deal with overthinking. While some extreme cases may require professional (even medical) help, most people who overthink can successfully tackle this tendency with the right holistic approach. Unfortunately, most books about overthinking overwhelm their readers with scientific explanations that may clarify the issue but don't necessarily contribute to solving it! That is why I decided to go straight to the point and give you seven practical, actionable strategies you can start implementing right away. Sure, we will discuss the possible causes of overthinking and its types beforehand so you can decide which strategies best fit your unique tendencies, but you won't find long technical explanations or medical jargon—I promise!

By tackling overthinking, you will find yourself with more mental clarity, leaving you space for the thoughts that really matter. You won't find yourself paralyzed when facing a decision or ruminating about past events that you can't change—or future scenarios that are equally beyond your control. You will experience improvement in every area of your life, from healthier relationships to higher self-esteem, and even your physical health will benefit. Overall, you will embrace a more peaceful, lighter, and happier life.

Are you excited about cleaning up your mind and getting rid of that excessive mental clutter that always gets in the way? Then, let's begin!

Understanding Why You Overthink

A person who thinks all the time has nothing to think about except thoughts, and so he loses touch with reality. –Alan Watts

Our friends make fun of us when we spend several minutes of indecision studying the wine list. We can relate to those romantic soap operas in which the main characters spend several months (or years!) grieving an old love that couldn't be.

We may get nervous thinking something terrible must have happened when our partner doesn't answer our text messages in a few hours. Like most people, we all overthink sometimes. But we don't overthink for the same reasons or in the same way.

How much thinking qualifies as overthinking, anyway? Don't we all spend a little too much time overthinking stuff now and then? Why do you overthink? Is it possible that the roots of your overthinking tendencies are in your childhood or even in your genetics?

Do you get any benefit from overthinking? Is worrying too much about the future the same as going over and over into details for fear of making a mistake?

In this introductory chapter, we will explore the concept of overthinking and some basic notions about the causes and different types of it. Learning this won't automatically make you stop overthinking, but it may help ease your mind and focus on the solutions ahead.

Let's Define Overthinking

The word itself gives us a hint: Overthinking is excessive thinking or thinking too much. But how much is *too* much? Simply said, while we may all spend some time and energy carefully considering every aspect of a situation before making a decision, regretting a past mistake, or worrying about a possible outcome, overthinking occurs when all those thoughts interfere with possible actions and affect our daily lives.

When you overthink, you struggle to focus your mind on anything else, as it becomes consumed by that one particular thing you keep thinking about over and over (Morin, 2024). And guess what? Contrary to popular belief, overthinking is not helpful in making the best decision or anticipating—and hopefully preventing—negative events. People who overthink can't easily relax. They feel mentally exhausted and second-guess their decisions, so they usually find themselves paralyzed or fearing the worst.

It would not be so bad if overthinking were only an occasional mishap. The problem is that it becomes a pattern: The brain gets used to creating these endless loops of thought, and then bam! You find yourself stuck. Overthinking becomes a habit that is hard to break. It becomes time-consuming and even takes a toll on your health.

This does not mean there is something wrong with you if you tend to overthink. Just like biting your nails is not a disease but makes you more likely to catch infections or hurt your fingers, overthinking is not a mental illness but can either be a symptom of one or make you more prone to specific health issues. Fortunately, for most people, overthinking can be addressed and treated with a series of holistic strategies we will approach in the following chapters.

How Frequent Is It?

If you have a stomachache one day, would you immediately make an appointment for gastric surgery? Is spending a whole night away synonymous with dealing with sleep disruptions? Is suffering a bad ankle sprint the same as having weak joints?

Not necessarily, right? Overthinking things from time to time doesn't mean you have an underlying mental health condition, although it may still affect your daily life, so it is worth addressing.

Most people overthink occasionally. In fact, overthinking is common up to the point that it is more frequent to overthink than to never experience it at all! Young people, in particular, struggle with their mental clutter.

According to research, if you are between 25 and 35 years old, there is an over 70% chance that you may experience overthinking. But it is not an exclusive tendency of millennials! If you are older, 45 to 55, you still have a 1 out of 2 chance to be an overthinker.

These results came out of a study conducted by sociologist Susan Nolen-Hoeksema, who interviewed 1,300 people. She found out that overthinking is dramatically frequent, but yes, it decreases with age, and only 1 out of 5 people in their 60s qualified as overthinkers (Camacho, 2024).

If you only occasionally second-guess decisions or take a long time to make a move, it doesn't mean you are an overthinker. It only becomes a problem when it affects your life. And if this is your case, you need to do something about it: You can't rely on aging to tackle the issue.

Common Underlying Causes

Why do some people overthink all the time, while others have no such tendency? What is behind this annoying and potentially harmful habit? Overthinking has different causes, and you may relate to one or more of them. Here are the predominant reasons:

- **Genetic factors:** You can inherit the tendency to overthink as other mental traits. This means that if your parents are overthinkers, you have more chances of being one yourself. "Genetic factors can also predispose a person to excessive thinking, which may show up when the person is faced with difficult situations" (Ramesh, 2022).

- **Childhood experiences:** If you learned to cope with problems by thinking about them as a child, you may find yourself stuck in this mechanism even when you are old enough to realize it is not useful. Sometimes, children learn these patterns by observing their parents—for example, if when you were growing up, your parents were constantly worried about losing their jobs or not making ends meet.

- **Stress:** People tend to overthink more when they are under stress. That is why learning to relax is a key to controlling overthinking. However, sometimes the mechanism serves a purpose: "While overthinking can cause stress, not all stress is bad. In the short term, having a lot of thoughts about a stressful situation can prompt you to make a move," explains Stephanie Anderson Witmer, from *GoodRx Health* (2023).

- **A traumatic event:** If you have experienced trauma, you may have your brain trapped in a state of hypervigilance. "When we're in potentially harmful situations, our fight, flight, or freeze reactions are primed and ready to go. As a result, those who have encountered traumatic situations may suffer from obsessive thoughts in such a context" (*What Causes Overthinking?* 2022).

- **Perfectionism:** If you are a perfectionist, chances are you also are an overthinker. "Perfectionists and overachievers have tendencies to overthink because of the fear of failing and the need to be perfect take over, which leads to replaying or criticizing decisions and mistakes," explains Dr. Sanam Hafeez, a neuropsychologist in New York City (Witmer, 2023).

- **Trying to control everything:** The illusion that we can control even the tiniest detail of our lives is sometimes the reason we overthink relationships, finances, health concerns, or future events. Of course, as a strategy, overthinking things beyond our control is ineffective. For example, thinking about a health concern can prompt you to book an appointment with your doctor and take the recommended tests, but you won't influence the *results* of such tests in any way.

- **Secondary gain:** Sometimes, people get used to overthinking because they receive some indirect benefit from it. For example, if your partner knows how much you worry, you may find yourself receiving extra reassurance from them. Additionally, if you are a procrastinator, by overthinking every decision or task, you may have found a way to postpone them indefinitely (Ramesh, 2022).

Finding out the causes of your particular overthinking tendencies may help you gain awareness and recognize your triggers. For example, if you realize you overthink when things are beyond your control, you can apply specific strategies to help you relax and practice acceptance to let go of that illusion.

On the other hand, if you realize you overthink because you are a perfectionist, you can apply other strategies, like setting specific time frames and "worry times."

In any case, remember that our goal is to work on how to cope with your overthinking tendencies. Others have dedicated thousands of pages to examine the science behind overthinking, including the role of neurotransmitters, hormones, and brain circuits. In my opinion, although science is fascinating, it doesn't necessarily bring you closer to actually dealing with your overthinking, so the rest of the chapters will focus on solutions, not so much on long, scientific explanations that don't necessarily help you work things out.

Not Everyone Overthinks the Same Way!

Martin, 18, spends several hours in front of the phone screen, unable to choose the best filter for his profile pic when creating an online resume. He carefully considers the effect such a picture will have on his chances of getting a job in the company of his dreams. "You are overthinking this, son," says Andrea, his mother, "Just pick one already!" She wonders how come his son is such a perfectionist without being aware of her own overthinking traits: Andrea usually stays asleep at night ruminating about her relationship with Martin's dad, wondering why the two of them couldn't make things work, and thinking how their marriage may have turned completely different... despite them being divorced for the past decade.

As you can see from the example above, overthinking can look very different for two people. Experts agree there are overthinking types, and most people can recognize themselves in one or more of them. Some have shortened the list to three main types—worrying, rumination, and overanalyzing (Wilding, 2024), and others have expanded this basic classification (Pugh, 2024). In any case, while there are many overthinkers out there, not all overthinkers are alike! As you study the following list of common overthinking types, see which one(s) better reflects your own traits.

Worrying

For this common type of overthinker, the future is a dangerous time. They keep worrying something bad may happen and constantly consider different unsettling scenarios: Maybe their partner will abandon them, or they will fail an important exam, catch a deadly virus, or an asteroid will crash on Earth, extinguishing human life...

In any case, these overthinkers may find themselves triggered not only by their daily worries but also by the constant overflow of negative news in digital media. There is no need to mention that although worrying to some degree about things that require your attention can help you accomplish goals and even prevent future problems, other things are completely beyond our control. "The uncertainty of what might happen, the potential for failure, and the fear of the unknown can make it a challenging form of overthinking" (Wilding, 2024).

"How on Earth am I going to do this?" "What if this [negative event] comes true?" If you often find yourself restless and agitated, can't enjoy your success because you start worrying about the next thing to come, or waste energy "preparing yourself" for every single worst scenario, you probably fall under this category.

Ruminating

Another common type of overthinking is getting caught in a loop where you remember past events, particularly those negative ones. "This can involve, for example, incessantly dwelling on a mistake you made in the past, or continuously replaying a time you were hurt over and over again in your mind" (*Overthinking: The 9 Different Types,* 2023). Those who overthink this way often experience regret, guilt, disappointment, bitterness, or self-criticism.

This type of overthinker may replay a breakup, an argument, or any kind of conflict over and over in their heads and spend hours wondering how things may have turned out if they had acted differently. They are caught up by their past, and that causes them difficulties in moving on, facing the future with optimism, or forgiving people for their past failures.

"I just can't believe she said that in front of my parents." "He might as well be dead! I will never forgive him for what he did to me." If you replay old conversations in your mind, feel resentment about episodes from the distant past, or feel not only that you can't forgive others but can't forgive yourself or accept a past mistake, then you are likely a ruminator.

Mind-Reading

A common type among people in the social anxiety spectrum is thinking what others are thinking. These overthinkers spend a lot of time trying to figure out other people's thoughts and opinions and spot hidden meanings behind every gesture or tone of voice. They may believe someone implied the opposite of what they actually said or wonder if there is a secret message behind their actions. As you can imagine, this type of overthinking is particularly detrimental to relationships.

Mind-readers often worry when they believe the other person said something negative about themselves or excessively engage in thinking about how others perceive them.

"What did she mean by that? Was she talking about me?" "Why is he staring?" "I am sure everyone thinks I'm a weirdo." If you spend more time thinking about what others think than actually listening to them and enjoying a conversation, you fall under this category of overthinker.

Indecisive

For this type of overthinker, you don't need to face a life-changing decision to engage in overthinking. They may spend a lot of time considering even small choices, such as their next holiday destination, what to wear on a date, or which friends they should invite to their birthday. "Having to make a choice of any sort throws your brain into overdrive," describes Angela Pugh from *Addiction Unlimited* in her podcast episode about overthinking (2024).

These overthinkers don't focus excessively on the past or the future but explore a specific topic to inconceivable levels of depth. "While this can sometimes lead to profound insights, more often than not, it results in getting bogged down in details that might not be particularly relevant," says Melody Wilding from the *Harvard Business Review* (2024).

They have a paralyzing fear of making the wrong choice, so they may take forever to consider every possible consequence of either choosing a or b.

As you can imagine, many times, not making a decision is a decision in itself, and that is how you may end up missing out on opportunities just because you didn't make up your mind when you had to.

Catastrophizing

Also known as over-reading into things, this type of overthinker tends to make a mountain out of a molehill. Basically, they exaggerate minor problems and imagine all kinds of negative consequences that could follow. Of course, these catastrophes are almost always non-existent, but the suffering they produce in the overthinker is real.

For example, a friend texts you while you are driving, and you tell yourself you will answer them later. Then, you come home and completely forget. Two days later, when you see their message, you start thinking about how you ruined the friendship, how they will never text you again, or even worse:

Maybe something terrible happened to them, and you were their only hope... In any case, this type of overthinker tends to blow everything out of proportion.

Hopeless Thoughts

Rather than imagining negative future outcomes as the catastrophizers above ("I am going to Mexico on vacation. What if there is an Earthquake while I am there?"), some overthinkers keep telling themselves there is simply nothing good ahead. Everything looks terrible, either for the future circumstances or for themselves. In the mentioned example, they may tell themselves there is no use in taking a vacation because there is no possible escape from their lousy life.

"I am beyond repair. No one can help me. There is no use in even trying." This is a dreadful type of overthinking that is deeply related to depression, so if you find yourself falling into this negative pattern over and over, you might want to consider professional help rather than relying only on the strategies we will see coming up.

Overgeneralizing

Overgeneralizing means taking an isolated event and turning it into a general rule. This type of overthinking happens when you experience failure or a setback; from it, you extrapolate information and tell yourself things are "always" a certain way or "never" as you want them to be. For example, if you don't get a promotion, you may spend hours telling yourself how your manager never appreciates you or how other people always get their way instead of you.

These overthinkers often view negative experiences as a pattern and assume one failure predicts ongoing failure in similar tasks (*Cognitive Distortions*, 2021). It usually includes negative self-talk, so it is directed with the following type of overthinking.

Beating Yourself Up

Together with a lack of confidence and low self-esteem, some overthinkers experience a constant loop of worthless thoughts about themselves. They keep punishing themselves for the slightest mistake and convince themselves they deserve that mistreatment. In their relationships, they keep looking for reassurance. "How can I be so stupid?" "I will never learn." "I am a terrible person. No wonder no one loves me." Does this ring a bell? It would be best if you worked hard to beat this constant mental punishment you put yourself through.

Mental Chatter

Maybe you spend a lot of time thinking about everyday details, even trivial things, but your brain goes on and on. Or, in the case of the so-called "big-picture overthinking" (Pugh, 2024), it is the opposite of that, and what keeps you up all night are huge interrogations, even existential questions, like your life purpose and such. In both cases, you keep having those long conversations with yourself that take you nowhere.

"Who am I?" "Am I really happy in this relationship?" "What is the meaning of life?" Although there is nothing inherently wrong in meditating about these matters once in a while, if they are interfering with your daily life, you should still attempt to control overthinking instead of being controlled by your endless train of thought. And it is nothing to be taken lightly: Although it may seem harmless, big-picture overthinking is related to existential depression (*Overthinking: The 9 Different Types,* 2023).

Now that we have seen them, you may relate to one or more types of overthinkers. Spotting those thoughts and recognizing their triggers is the first step to learning how to cope with your overthinking tendencies and keep them from affecting your life and well-being.

Key Takeaways

We have seen what overthinking is—and what it is not; how frequent it is, especially among young people; and some of the possible reasons you are an overthinker. We have also explored different ways people overthink. This is what you should remember the most:

- We all overthink sometimes, but it becomes a problem when it consumes our time and energy and interferes with our lives.

- Overthinking is not a mental illness but a habit, and as such, it can be corrected with the proper training.

- Overthinking is likely multicausal, as genetic inheritance, certain personality traits, observation, and past experiences, along with stress, play a role.

- Similarly, we don't all overthink in the same ways.

Understanding that overthinking is frequent and recognizing your type and possible causes will help you ease your worries and focus on solutions. The following chapters will provide different strategies you can apply—starting today.

Strategy #1:

Your Body as the Gatekeeper

A fit body, a calm mind, a house full of love. These things cannot be bought—they must be earned. –Naval Ravikant

We have mentioned how overthinking is not a disease but a habit. In any case, it is a negative one that affects your physical and mental health in many different ways. The first thing we need to break from a bad habit is not to force ourselves to stop (if only it were that easy!) but to replace it with other healthier habits.

As we will see in this chapter, overthinking is not "all in your head" but in your body as well—so taking care of your body will help you achieve a healthier mind and keep those overthinking symptoms under control.

How Your Body Displays Overthinking Symptoms

Look at your hands. You may be tempted to consider them possessions, something you own and control (after all, you can move them at will to scroll down the screen or sweep the floor). But they are a part of you: You are not simply a mind trapped inside a body. You *are* that body! Mind, body, and spirit are a single unit. When we accept that, it should not surprise us that our thoughts, especially the negative loops of overthinking, have physical effects on us.

Let's see how overthinking impacts our physical health:

- **High blood pressure:** According to Dr. Narayan Gadkar, a cardiologist, overthinking increases your chances of developing chronic stress, making you more susceptible to heart problems: "High stress means high cholesterol levels, and you may also adopt unhealthy habits such as smoking and alcohol consumption that can create havoc on your overall well-being" (Gupta, 2022).

- **Poor sleep quality:** Both our bodies and minds need a proper night's rest to recover from their daily efforts, heal from wounds and diseases, and properly store everything we have learned. However, this doesn't happen when we are chronic overthinkers. "Ruminating on almost everything and worrying constantly about things over which you have little or no control often lead to fewer hours of sleep. Thus, overthinking impairs your quality of sleep and may make you cranky the next day" (Toshi, 2024).

- **Digestive issues:** Do you find yourself so worried or engaged in overthinking that you skip a meal or take only a few bites? This happens because your brain is so busy that it ignores hunger signals. For other people, overthinking causes them to overeat because of anxiety. Both of them are negative for your well-being. And that is not all! Even if you manage to eat well, you may not be able to digest your food properly. "Stress due to overthinking results in gastrointestinal problems such as inflammatory bowel disease (IBD), or even irritable bowel syndrome (IBS)" (Gupta, 2022).

- **Headaches:** This is perhaps one of the most frequent and noticeable symptoms of stress. Worrying, ruminating, and thinking too hard can cause tension headaches that make it hard to go through with your daily activities.

- **Muscular tension:** Similarly, tension can accumulate in other muscles. You may suffer from back pain, a stiff neck, or pain and spasms in other parts of your body.

We can easily see how our thoughts affect our bodies and why we must address overthinking if we don't want to pay for it with our health. That is why taking care of our bodies is the first strategy: It will also have a soothing effect on our minds.

The Positive Impact of Physical Activity

First of all, you should understand the purpose of making physical activity a part of your daily routine. You can't get out of your head, but you can—and must!—get off your couch.

Being physically active has tons of benefits for your health and counteracts many of the negative effects of overthinking. Exercise reduces your blood pressure, helps you sleep better, relaxes you, and boosts your appetite.

Most importantly, there is a clear relationship between being physically active and mentally healthy. When you exercise, your brain releases endorphins, or "feel-good" hormones. Physical activities also give you opportunities for socializing, which is great for distracting you from all those endless ruminations and worries. It is easier to focus on the present time and sensations when you are moving your body! Plus, planning your workouts and being consistent help you increase your self-confidence and stop specific types of overthinking, like beating yourself up: "When you accomplish your fitness goals, you'll start to believe in yourself and your ability to overcome obstacles—a fantastic way to stop overthinking" (*Tools to Stop Overthinking*, n.d.).

What is the best type of exercise to reduce overthinking? It depends a lot on your personal preferences and possibilities according to your current fitness level. Additionally, it might be up to your particular type of overthinking. For instance, if you fall into the mind-reading type and have social anxiety, playing a sports team may not be the best choice. In any case, here are some recommended physical exercises for calming the mind:

- **Yoga:** This is the perfect low-impact method to heal your body and mind. It typically involves controlled breathing, physical postures (asanas), and meditation exercises.

- **Walking:** Walking is the most simple yet effective exercise you can engage in daily as part of your routine. You can walk at your own pace, which means you will still notice benefits even if you are not perfectly fit.

- **Hiking:** This activity involves aerobic exercise and being outdoors. As we'll see later, spending time in nature offers all kinds of physical and mental benefits, and it is definitely recommended to control your overthinking.

- **Swimming:** Swimming is another powerful aerobic exercise suitable for any age or body type. Being in warm water is relaxing and helps you achieve better sleep quality, as well as alleviate muscular tensions.

- **Dancing:** This is another aerobic exercise you can enjoy, and it's particularly helpful for socializing. You get to meet new people with your interests and have a lot of fun! And you don't need to be good at dancing to enjoy or benefit from this physical activity.

- **Strength training:** Lifting weights and building muscles is not for everyone, but if you need to boost your self-esteem and gain more confidence, this could be the right exercise for you.

Detox Your Organism as Well

You know how overthinking feels like having a cluttered mind and how you need a mind cleanse. But you may wonder what you need to eat (or refrain from eating) has anything to do with it. What does food have to do with your thoughts anyway? You need to detox your mind, yes, but would it have any impact to detox your body as well? It is curious, but indeed it would!

According to research from an emerging medical field called nutritional psychiatry, what we eat directly impacts our mental well-being. These experts suggest anti-anxiety diets because they recognize the gut and the brain—though physically apart in our bodies—have a close, intimate relationship. "The gut and the brain are in constant conversation about digestion, appetite—and even your mood" (Soong, 2024). Scientists may even talk about the gut as a "second brain."

The connection has two aspects: First, there is the vagus nerve, "which starts in the brain and extends through the abdomen and intestines" (Soong, 2024) and explains the motives because people experience stomach aches and digestive issues when they are anxious. Second, there is the neurotransmitter serotonin, which affects mood and is produced in the intestines. With that knowledge, we can't emphasize enough the importance of a healthy, balanced diet and proper hydration to support brain health, optimize its functions, and reduce anxiety. Here is how to eat to feel mentally better and keep overthinking under control:

- **Don't skip meals:** Having your meals at regular times keeps your blood sugar levels steady, which prevents energy lows. If you are not used to having breakfast in the morning, starting this habit (and, if possible, including some protein) will make you begin the day with more energy.

- **Increase whole foods and reduce refined carbohydrates:** Uma Naidoo, director of nutritional and lifestyle psychiatry at Massachusetts General Hospital, emphasizes the importance of eating fruits, vegetables, legumes, and unprocessed grains because of their positive impact on your gut. Conversely, you should refrain from refined wheat flour (reduce your white bread, pizza, and pasta intake), foods with added sugars or artificial sweeteners, deep-fried foods, and packaged snacks (Soong, 2024).

- **Include omega-3 and antioxidants:** Omega-3-rich foods such as salmon, sardines, or other fish contain fatty oils that "regulate neurotransmitters, reduce inflammation, and promote healthy brain function" (Chrichton-Stuart & Dias, 2024). Other foods are recommended because they contain amino acids, minerals, and antioxidants. Include eggs, yogurt, chamomile tea, dark chocolate, avocados, Brazil nuts, and leafy greens on your plate.

- **Avoid caffeine and alcohol:** Staying hydrated is essential for your well-being, and even mild dehydration may affect your mood. However, you shouldn't pour just anything on your glass. Alcoholic drinks may seem to have a relaxing effect, but once the alcohol is processed in your body, it makes you edgy and interferes with sleep. And speaking of sleep, that is why you should refrain from caffeine as well, not only in coffee but in sodas and energy drinks as well. "They can make you feel jittery and nervous and can interfere with sleep" (Sawchuk, 2017).

Nature, the Best Therapist!

During 2020, Sara was socially distancing from friends and family, working remotely, and leaving the house only to take short trips to the grocery store. Like it happened to many others, the pandemic and the subsequent lockdown were affecting her mental health. Luckily for Sarah, she discovered the advantages of weekend camping trips. "I felt the difference almost immediately—out in the woods, I wasn't scrambling for my phone or thinking about work deadlines," she explains.

Without being aware of the many evidence researchers and health care providers had already of the benefits of spending time in nature, Sara felt these benefits firsthand: "My attention span seemed to lengthen and level out. I relaxed. I came home feeling rested and a little more cheerful, and these trips became a way to manage the stress of the pandemic" (Youngblood Gregory, 2024).

If you feel like you can't get out of your head, maybe the answer is simple: Get out. For a long time, science has found a strong correlation between mental health and spending time in nature. It is not such a big surprise: Despite living in a technological society where the predominant view is screens of all shapes and sizes, we are still the descendants of our hunter-gatherer ancestors, whose brains were wired for outdoor life. According to Mayo Clinic nurse practitioner Jodie M. Smith, as little as five minutes of being exposed to nature contributes to regulating our sympathetic nervous system. Immersion in nature is part of many programs to handle chronic mental illnesses such as depression, anxiety, post-traumatic stress disorder (PTSD), and attention-deficit/hyperactivity disorder (ADHD) (Youngblood Gregory, 2024).

Additionally, being outdoors is proven to increase memory, cognitive ability, and problem-solving skills, better manage emotions, and improve sleep quality. "Daily exposure to natural light helps regulate sleep/wake cycles. By making sure that you get outside in sunlight every day, you can improve your ability to sleep at night" (*3 Ways Getting Outside*, 2023).

Some types of overthinkers get the most advantage of forest bathing:

- If you suffer from hopeless thoughts or are beating yourself up, take a long walk through the forest, as research shows that a 90-minute walk in nature decreases activity in the area of the brain linked to negative thoughts (American Heart Association, 2024).

- If you fall into the category of indecisive overthinkers, consider how changing your scenery boosts your creativity and can help you improve your problem-solving skills.

- And if you belong to the big-picture overthinkers, and you get lost in general, wondering about the meaning of life or your purpose in this world, "a dose of awe might remind you just how wondrous the world is. Nature provides trees that were hundreds of years old before you were even born, towering mountains that touch the clouds, and a sky full of uncountable stars" (American Heart Association, 2024).

No matter what type of chronic overthinker you may be, going outdoors and spending time in nature is part of the strategy for being physically healthy and keeping this tendency under control.

Here are some ideas of activities in nature you can include as part of your plan:

- **Take a walk whenever you can:** Leave the car keys at home and walk when you need to get some groceries or even go to work.

- **Use the bike:** If you need to commute short distances, choose the bicycle. Not only is it a great way to exercise, but you also get to breathe fresh air and enjoy some much-needed sunlight.

- **Go on a picnic:** Nature offers many options for socializing. "Time in nature can help with your personal relationships, too. Natural beauty results in more prosocial behaviors, like generosity and empathy" (American Heart Association, 2024). The best part is that you don't need access to an immense wild area. You can benefit from spending an afternoon at your local park surrounded by trees.

- **Take advantage of your outdoor area at home:** If you have a small garden, patio, backyard, or even a small balcony, take frequent breaks from the screens and go outside. Gardening, working out in a green area, or simply enjoying a view of the sky while you sip your tea can do wonders for your mental well-being.

Key Takeaways

We have learned why taking care of your body is the first strategy to achieving a healthy mind—which, of course, includes controlling your overthinking. This tendency is not only in your head; it manifests as a series of physical symptoms. This is what you should do:

- Engage in regular physical activity, choosing the exercise routine that suits your preferences, current physical state, and particular overthinking traits.

- Consider the link between your brain and your gut. Then eat accordingly!

- Make sure you spend some time outdoors every week—if possible, every day—to reap the mental health benefits of nature.

Your body is not something you possess; it is an integral part of yourself as a being. Fortunately, the better you take care of your body, the better your mind will feel as well. Perhaps there is not a more obvious connection between mind and body than our breath. Breathing connects us with the present moment and calms our thoughts. That is why breathing techniques are a major strategy for overcoming overthinking. We will further expand on their importance in the following chapter.

Strategy #2:

Mindfulness and Meditation

Wherever you are, be there totally. –Eckhart Tolle

What is it about overthinking that makes us miserable? Why does it affect our everyday lives in so many aspects? It's mostly because when you are riding on an endless train of thought, you are lost. Your body may remain in a place, but your conscience is removed and misses out. This becomes particularly obvious when you ruminate or worry: You are losing the present moment. Luckily, there's always a way back. In this sense, mindfulness and meditation help you reconnect and calm the turbulent waters of your overthinking mind.

How Mindfulness Works

Our minds have the amazing ability to wander from the past to the future (sometimes revolving around scenarios without any base in reality), solve all kinds of problems, and look at things from different perspectives. However, one thing our minds often fail at is staying still! If we leave our thoughts unattended, they get tangled and trap us in their intricacy. The average person has about 70,000 daily thoughts, which isn't exactly good news. "A busy mind typically leads to anger, rage, sadness, and insecurity. With thousands of thoughts racing through our minds, it's hard to make decisions, have connected conversations, and handle our emotions" (McGregor, 2018). Nonetheless, we still retain the innate ability to be aware of our inner state and our current surroundings. To do this, we need to control our minds instead of leaving them unattended. The practice of mindfulness is "kind of like becoming a parent to your mind rather than letting it control you," explains Crystal Hoshaw from *Healthline*. She adds, "In the end, the mind is simply a willful toddler" (2022).

Mindfulness is the name of the simple, everyday techniques aimed at gently redirecting your awareness to your present state and the moment you're living. When you are mindful, it's not that you stop thinking, but you remove the negative connotations of those thoughts. With mindfulness, you learn to recognize your thoughts and feelings and get to observe them as they are, accepting them without judgment.

It's not a complex technique you have to master but something already available to you. "Mindfulness is a quality that every human being already possesses, it's not something you have to conjure up, you just have to learn how to access it" (Mindful, 2020). Practicing mindfulness means becoming more aware and gaining the ability to turn your focus to the present circumstances. The more you practice mindfulness, the easier you accomplish it and the calmer your mind gets.

By applying some specific meditation techniques or inserting short pauses of awareness during your everyday activities, regular practices of mindfulness have many benefits for your well-being, including the following:

- reduced stress

- increased awareness

- improved cognitive ability

- better pain management

- relief from physical symptoms like stomach problems and headaches

- boosted the immune system

- improved life quality

Practicing mindfulness is said to be simple but not easy, especially if you are a chronic overthinker whose mind usually wanders all the time. The key is being persistent in your practice. Remember: There's no wrong way of doing it, and you will notice some benefits for at least trying.

The Power of Grounding and Other Simple Techniques

With enough practice, mindfulness can become a part of your routine. It's a powerful resource you can access whenever you need to calm your mind. But how do you begin? The simplest exercise is to focus on your breathing. Here's how:

1. If you are in a safe place, close your eyes. Turn your attention to how air comes in and out through your nose. Does it feel cold or warm? Does it make any sound? Don't try to change the breathing pattern. Simply observe it.

2. You may feel your mind pulling you toward another thought. That's okay. Observe the thought and let it go.

3. Focus again on your breath. By simply putting your attention in your breath, your mind slows down, and the overwhelming number of thoughts decreases.

Let's explore some more common mindfulness techniques you can start applying today:

The Body Scan

The ability to hear, understand, and respond to our internal sensations of the body is called interoceptive awareness. Research shows a connection between high levels of overthinking and low levels of interoceptive awareness. "When we're disconnected from physical, internal signals, we overthink in an attempt to find answers that the body already knows. Practicing mindfulness of the body is just one way to quiet the mind." (Conway, 2020). Here's how you do it:

1. Go to a calm, safe space. Once there, sit upright or lie down on your back.

2. If possible, close your eyes to avoid distractions and turn your full attention inward.

3. Extend your legs and arms at your sights. If you're lying down, face your palms upward.

4. Focus all of your attention on your toes and feet. Notice if there are any sensations.

5. Observe if you can distinguish temperature, tension, tingling, discomfort, or anything else—don't judge these sensations; there are no wrong answers.

6. Perceive if a sensation changes as you observe it.

7. Notice the kind of feelings the sensation provokes. Do you experience attachment or aversion?

8. Move your focus upward to the next body part (your legs) and repeat.

9. Slowly and consciously scan all your body parts up to the head.

The Five Senses

This is a quick, effective exercise to help you reconnect with the present moment when you can't sleep or are overwhelmed with thoughts. The best part is you can do it anywhere, even if you are on public transport on your way to work or in the middle of a crowded classroom.

1. Notice five things you can see. Give your full attention to each object and take a few deep breaths before moving to the next one.

2. Now, notice four things you can feel. Again, focus your attention on each sensation.

3. Notice three things you can hear.

4. Notice two things you can smell.

5. Notice one thing you can taste.

Grounding

Also known as earthing, this technique is based on making direct skin contact with the Earth's natural surfaces, such as sand, soil, grass, or water. There are many ways to achieve this, such as the following:

- Go outside and stand on the ground barefoot.

- Practice gardening or simply touch humid soil, sand, or grass with your bare hands.

- Lie flat on the grass.

- Submerge yourself in a natural body of water—the ocean, a lake, a river, or a pond.

- If indoors, put your hands into water and focus on the sensations. Don't assign values to them. Observe, don't judge.

The practice of grounding is supposed to connect a person's energy with the Earth's magnetic field. Although there is little scientific research to back that belief (Bence, 2024), it is still a good practice for reducing stress and calming overwhelming thoughts because it connects us with the present moment.

Practice grounding techniques even when you are calm. This will make it easier to use those same exercises in difficult times when you need to cope with stress. When you are experiencing distressing thoughts, Crystal Raypole, from *Healthline*, recommends rating from one to ten your levels of distress before and after each exercise: "What level is your distress when you begin? How much did it decrease after the exercise? This can help you get a better idea of whether a particular technique is working for you" (2024).

Walking Meditation

Some people find it particularly challenging to focus on their sensations while sitting still or lying down. If this is the case for you, and you feel your overthinking becomes worse than ever, you may find it easier to meditate in motion. Here's an exercise you can put into practice even indoors (Mayo Clinic, 2022):

1. Go to a quiet place 10 to 20 feet in length. Ideally, it should be outside, surrounded by nature, but it can also be a hall in your building, a terrace, or a garage.

2. Begin to walk that distance slowly.

3. Focus on the experience of walking. Bring awareness to each sensation: how your body stands and which subtle movements it performs to keep your balance.

4. Once you reach the end of the path, simply turn around and keep walking.

Everyday Meditation

Meditation is not a single practice but a family of activities. In this sense, Dr. Richard J. Davidson, a neuroscientist from the University of Wisconsin, compares the meaning of the word "meditation" in the Buddhist tradition to the meaning of "sports" for the average American today (*Meditation 101*, 2019). Just like different sports require the use of different muscles and abilities, each meditation technique requires a different mental skill.

All forms of meditation have a goal in common: The purpose is to bring clarity and awareness by purposely observing our thoughts, or to be more precise, the "space" between those thoughts. As we do, we gain awareness and realize we aren't our minds; we aren't those thoughts, and, therefore, they lose part of the power over us. By regularly meditating, people experience many benefits, including lower blood pressure, lower heart rate, less perspiration, less anxiety, lower levels of cortisol, slower breathing, and overall more feelings of well-being (*Meditation 101*, 2019).

However, in our busy Western world, we may find it impossible to sit still and "empty our minds." We may believe the only way to achieve this state is by spending a lot of money on devices like meditation mats, chairs, cushions; brain-sensing headbands; Tibetan bowls; or apps that can guide us step by step. Some people give up on meditation before even trying because they say they lack the time. However, we can practice brief, simple techniques at home to receive the many benefits of meditation. Here are two you can make part of your routine or use in specific moments when they need to calm your thoughts:

Step-By-Step Meditation for Beginners

Meditation is more straightforward than you may believe... and harder at the same time! This shouldn't keep you from practicing it. Go over the following steps, then put down the book and start today:

1. Sit down somewhere calm and comfortable. It can be on a chair or the floor.

2. Set a timer. Some people worry they'll lose themselves in the meditation and that the practice may get in the way of their other activities. To avoid this, simply set a time limit and program your phone's alarm. It doesn't need to be too long; five to ten minutes is enough.

3. Begin focusing on your body. Which position did you choose for sitting? Are your legs crossed? Do your feet touch the floor? Make sure the position is stable and comfortable so you can stay like that for a while.

4. Focus on your breath. Feel the sensation of the air going in and out of your body, through your nose. Don't try to control the pace; just observe it.

5. Notice the wandering of your mind. Your attention will inevitably move away from your breath to other places. Just notice it and calmly return it to your breath.

6. Practice kindness. Don't judge yourself or your wandering thoughts. Let them go and come back.

7. Repeat the previous three steps as many times as you want: Focus on your breath, observe the wandering mind, and gently bring your attention back to the breath. Do it calmly again and again.

8. When you feel ready, slowly open your eyes or lift your gaze. Notice your surroundings and any sound in the environment. Observe how your body feels right now. Notice your thoughts and emotions as you gently end the exercise.

Focused Meditation

This is another technique that can be particularly useful for people who find it too hard to focus on their breath or inner sensations. The goal is to anchor your focus to a single element without thinking or judging. The idea is basically the same: "Staying in the present moment, circumventing the constant stream of commentary from your conscious mind, and allowing yourself to slip into an altered state of consciousness" (Scott, 2024).

Just like in the previous dynamic, you should sit comfortably in a quiet area, set a time frame you're okay with, and direct your focus to your element of choice.

In this case, your entire attention should be on something, either an object, a sound, or even a concept. Here are some ideas:

- **Visuals:** You can look at the flame of a candle, the branch of a tree moving in the wind, a painting, a statue, a body of water, etc.

- **Sounds:** You can play a track of windchimes, bells, or singing bowls; listen to a metronome; or focus on a single environmental sound, like a bird chirping.

- **Concepts:** Embrace compassion, gratitude, or acceptance as the center of your meditative practice.

The most powerful benefits of meditation don't come from long sessions but from being constant with your practice. Embrace it as a new habit, and try to do it every day at a regular time (for example, before having breakfast early in the morning or before bedtime). Leave yourself reminders around the house, or set an alarm for your meditation session so you find it easier to stick to it.

The key to successfully meditating is being consistent. The more regularly you practice, even for five minutes a day, the easier it will become to maintain your focus for longer, and the more you'll notice its benefits.

Key Takeaways

We've learned that the main reason overthinking makes us miserable is that it robs us of the present moment. When we allow our minds to wander uncontrollably, they turn to the past and the future or create non-existent scenarios. We can increase our mindfulness and gain awareness of the here and now by applying meditation techniques.

- Mindfulness isn't something we should learn but cultivate, as it's already within us.

- Practicing mindfulness and meditation offers many benefits for our mental and physical health.

- You don't need to spend money on gadgets or even apps. You can begin meditating with simple techniques at home.

- It's normal for the mind to wander while you meditate. Remember to simply observe those thoughts and feelings, not to judge them.

- The most basic technique to stop your mind from wandering is to focus on your breath.

- Meditation provides powerful benefits with regular practice. The more you make a habit out of it, the easier it will become.

Although quieting your mind is an excellent strategy for controlling your overthinking, you will still experience overwhelming thoughts sometimes. On these occasions, you need to address those thoughts to learn how to redirect them, as we'll see in the following chapter.

Strategy #3:

The Cognitive Restructuring

Whether you think you can, or you think you can't—you're right. – Henry Ford

According to Jennice Vilhauer, a psychologist in Los Angeles, although many random events in life are beyond our control (as well as the reactions from others), we *do* control how we perceive, interpret, and think about those events. They generate specific feelings, but we respond to such feelings with a behavior: "No one can choose your thoughts or actions; those are yours alone" (2020).

If our thoughts were just thoughts and remained there, it wouldn't be much of a problem. But, as the epigraph of Henry Ford that opens this chapter reminds us, our thoughts play a role in shaping our reality. This isn't true for all cases, of course. I'm telling you, catastrophizers who read me, no, you won't "cause" your lab results to come back positive because you spent last night worrying about them. And chances are that if your partner didn't call you back, it was because they were stuck in traffic, not because they were involved in a fatal car crash.

On the other hand, think about how considering yourself a failure before taking an exam or going to a job interview makes it more likely to make a mistake or give up even before trying! Cognitive behavioral therapy (CBT) is a form of psychological treatment used for addressing several mental issues, such as anxiety, depression, substance abuse, relationship problems, eating disorders, and other mental illnesses. The core of this approach is understanding psychological problems as the product of unhelpful thinking, learned patterns, and behavior (American Psychological Association, 2017). CBT offers many benefits, as it helps patients become aware of their negative patterns of thought and how they affect their feelings and moods. Treatments are usually short and effective, and some people see results in 5 to 20 sessions. It's also more affordable than other types of therapy and can help patients gain valuable coping skills without the use of medication (Cherry, 2023a).

That's why this third strategy will involve implementing CBD techniques in your everyday life. CBD offers an interesting approach to controlling overthinking, allowing you to observe, modify, and redirect your thoughts. Let's get to it!

Recognizing Your Cognitive Distortions

As we established earlier, we get to choose our thoughts. And what happens after we have chosen them? Most times, we stick to them as if they were facts. "Your thoughts, if you think them over and over and assign truth to them, become beliefs," explains Vilhauer, and adds that those same beliefs we hold on to create a cognitive lens through which we interpret the events of our world. "This lens serves as a selective filter through which you sift the environment for evidence that matches up with what you believe to be true" (2020).

Your brain is wired to work on a selective filtering system and create shortcuts to avoid an overload of information. It can't work properly with evidence contrary to a specific belief, so it dismisses it. For example, if you are convinced conspiracies are real, you'll find evidence of them everywhere. If you are religious, you'll see the presence of the divine, whereas other people simply see random events. And if you keep telling yourself you are a complete failure... guess what?

You are likely to put yourself in situations that will confirm your belief—and, oh, surprise! You'll fail more times than not. If you systematically fall into an inadequate thinking pattern, those negative thoughts become beliefs. And what happens when you stick to these negative beliefs and see the world through this bias? You get yourself a cognitive distortion, like a funhouse mirror that distorts whatever you place in front of them. "These unhelpful filters make whatever life circumstances we find ourselves in that much more anxiety-provoking and challenging," explains Dr. Peter Grinspoon from Harvard Medical School (2022).

There are many types of cognitive distortions, and some of them overlap with one another. Here, we'll see examples of the most common ones. Can you spot any in yourself?

- **All-or-nothing thinking:** This filter means seeing everything in absolute terms, as black or white. For example, you have stuck with the habit of meditating daily for the past two weeks, but last night, you fell asleep before you could meditate. "See, I can't commit to meditating," you tell yourself, and stop practicing altogether.

- **Overgeneralization:** As we've seen in Chapter 1, this means taking an isolated negative event and turning it into a pattern of hopelessness. For example, you get rejected in a job interview, and you tell yourself you'll *never* get a job.

- **Personalization:** This filter leads you to blame yourself for anything negative that happens and makes everything about you. For example, your mom receives bad news at the doctor's appointment, and you blame yourself for not being there with her, or the soccer team you're in loses a match, and you think it's your fault despite there being 10 other players.

- **Filtering:** This means focusing on a single aspect of a situation and dwelling on the negative side. For example, you write a short story and read it to your classmates. Six of them congratulate you, and the seventh person gives you some constructive criticism. Disregarding all the positive feedback, you tell yourself: "I knew nobody would like it. I suck as a writer!"

- **Emotional reasoning:** This happens when you mistake your feelings for reality. If you are jealous, that means your partner "must be cheating" on you. Or, if you feel lonely, you may say to yourself, "Nobody likes me" despite having friends. Basically, you take emotions as facts.

Challenge Your Beliefs

So, how can you, as an overthinker, break free from cognitive distortion that deeply affects how you feel and see your reality? In other words, how can we remove that funhouse mirror from our minds? Becoming aware of your cognitive distortions is the first step to overcoming them. If those beliefs are too firmly installed, you may need to refer to a professional therapist who can help you spot them. However, sometimes, you can achieve awareness through mindfulness or journaling.

One key for spotting cognitive distortions is noticing certain indicators in your thoughts: Words such as "all," "never," and "always" usually point toward generalization—and don't withstand simple reasoning. Perhaps you didn't get *this* job, but does it mean you'll *never* get one? That's right, you're overgeneralizing! Like failing in an interview wasn't bad enough, you are punishing yourself with a cognitive distortion. And as it usually happens, the thought is responsible for the discomfort more than the situation itself. Once you've spotted a negative thought, the following step is to challenge yourself. Focus on gathering evidence that contradicts your thought. For example, you tell yourself that nobody likes you. Nobody? Really? Not even your mom? How about your best friend from high school who moved abroad but still texts you every week?

As you realize the thought doesn't correlate with reality, you may observe the emotion behind the idea is still real. What do you feel when you tell yourself you'll never get a job? You are frustrated. Name that emotion and use that to replace your generalization: "I'm frustrated because I didn't get this job." Or, state the loneliness: "I know some people like me, but I have none of them around right now, and I feel lonely."

Finally, do the exercise of saying the thought out loud and consider whether you'd say something like that to a friend of yours. Your favorite outfit may no longer fit you, and you say, "I'm a whale." Would you say that to a friend? I bet you wouldn't, no matter how much weight they gained. So, why would you say it to yourself? Get used to treating yourself as you would treat your friends. That will make you realize how much of that negative self-talk can—and should—be reformulated.

Reframing Negative Thoughts

We have seen how our brains stick to our thoughts. The more you cling to a negative thought, the more likely it is to become a belief and generate a cognitive distortion. Similarly, when you adopt a positive mindset, you'll be more open to finding evidence that supports this new state of mind—hence, you'll live in a happier reality! Is there a way to prevent so much negative thinking in the first place?

Here are some practical strategies you can adopt starting today:

- **Practice positive affirmations:** By repeating positive thoughts, you can slowly gain positive beliefs. "I am worthy of love," "I am resilient and have the strength to overcome challenges," "There's so much good in life."

- **Rephrase your criticism:** Substitute negative thoughts with neutral thoughts. For example, if someone doesn't smile back at you in the office, instead of thinking, "Wow, they are rude," or "I bet they hate me," say to yourself, "They must be having a bad day."

- **Embrace gratitude:** Adopt the habit of feeling thankful for the good things in your life. Challenge yourself to find at least three positive aspects in every situation. "It might not feel natural, but eventually, it may become a spontaneous habit" (Silva Casabianca, 2022). You crashed your car? Of course, it's terrible news, but think about how good it is your insurance policy is paid, that no one got hurt, and that your child wasn't there with you at the time of the accident.

- **Implement visualization techniques:** Whenever you experience negative thinking, visualize a giant red stop sign. The more you get used to it, the faster you'll be able to recognize these thoughts and prevent them from escalating.

Keys for Cognitive Restructuring

Also known as cognitive reframing, cognitive restructuring is a series of techniques CBT uses to change unhealthy beliefs and negative thoughts to improve your well-being and mental health. You deconstruct all those negative beliefs and rebuild them in a balanced and more accurate way. Most people find it helpful to work with a therapist, although anyone can use the techniques to improve their thinking habits. Here are some strategies:

Thought Records

The most challenging part is recognizing the negative thoughts. Journaling or even saying them out loud may help you identify them. When you do, make sure you list the situation that triggered the thought and the emotions it provoked. For example:

- **Situation:** My teenage daughter rolled her eyes when I told her to study harder.

- **Thought:** She never listens to me. She doesn't respect me anymore.

- **Emotion:** Frustration, sadness, anger.

- Next, gather evidence for and against your thought and use it to develop a more balanced thought.

- **Evidence in favor:** She doesn't want to hang out with me very often. She seems distant. She complains when I ask her to do stuff.

- **Evidence against:** She is getting good grades at school, and she studies—despite complaining about it.

- **Balanced thought:** She may not like to be told to study, but she does listen. Some rebelling is a natural part of adolescence.

Keeping a record of your thoughts on a period—for example, one month—may help you recognize recurrent negative patterns.

Socratic Questioning

This is a useful technique for recognizing if your thoughts are based on real evidence or, on the contrary, are illogical or biased. Consider one of your thoughts and ask yourself the following questions (Ackerman, 2018):

1. Is this a realistic thought?

2. Am I basing this thought on facts or emotions?

3. How could I test this belief?

4. What is the evidence for this thought? Could I be misinterpreting it?

5. Is this a thought I have out of habit?

6. Is the situation really black or white? Or am I missing some shades?

Behavioral Experiments and Role-Playing

A way to challenge your thoughts and beliefs is by testing them out in real-life situations. Such an experiment is designed with the help of a therapist with the specific purpose of challenging a core belief. Do you always label strangers as rude and unkind?

You could test this belief by asking a small favor of someone you've never seen before and observing their responses and reactions.

Another example is if you believe your teenage daughter never listens to you. The experiment could involve you telling her a story she can relate to and, some days later, bringing up the topic once more to see if she remembers what you said. The evidence you gather could refute your core belief and help you change it to a more accurate one.

Another technique used by CBT therapists is when they act like the other person to represent a situation that triggers or puts to test your negative thinking. You act like yourself and are encouraged to respond as you would usually do.

However, this technique isn't as simple to use without the help of a professional.

Key Takeaways

Our brains are responsible for turning recurrent thoughts into beliefs, which shape our reality as they lead us to focus on evidence confirming them and disregard facts that contradict them. These beliefs can form cognitive distortions that negatively affect our daily lives.

CBT offers strategies and approaches for restructuring our thoughts and reframing our beliefs into more accurate and balanced ones. Here are the main points to remember:

- You can't control external events or other people's reactions, but you can choose your thoughts.

- Emotions aren't a good base for reasoning. Always challenge your beliefs with facts.

- Journaling and thought records are great tools for gaining awareness of your thoughts.

- Make the habit of actively choosing positive thoughts.

This strategy we have seen is great for people who tend to overanalyze or be too harsh on themselves. What if you ruminate about the past or worry too much about possible future events? Then, the strategy we'll see next is the right approach for you.

Strategy #4:

Declutter Your Mental Load

If you must look back, do so forgivingly. If you must look forward, do so prayerfully. However, the wisest thing you can do is be present in the present... Gratefully. –Maya Angelou

Some time ago, I went to my nephew's wedding. He's a kind young man who fell in love with a woman he met at work. The wedding was lovely, and the couple looked on top of the world. I was having a lot of fun like the other guests... except for the groom's mom, Martha, my sister-in-law, who seemed upset. I approached her and asked her if something was wrong, as everything seemed to be going on so well. "Oh, it's nothing," she said, "It's just that they look so perfect for each other right now, but I keep wondering, what if they can't make it through all the struggles of married life and end up getting a divorce? What if they want to conceive but discover they can't have children? Or, what if she cheats on him? That would break my son's heart!"

As you can see, although nothing in the moment of the wedding indicated things could go wrong in the future, and everyone was enjoying the happy occasion, Martha's worries interfered with her happiness. By overthinking ways the marriage could go wrong, she missed out on her son's wedding—a once-in-a-lifetime occasion!

I felt sorry for Martha then, but I know she isn't the only one. I bet many of us overthinkers can relate because we've all missed out on a special occasion. After all, we tend to ruminate about the past—or worry about the future. These are two frequent ways in which overthinking manifests, but both are beyond your control; letting go is the key to living a plentiful life anchored in the present. This is what we'll work on through this strategy.

How to Stop Rumination

Although we may all overthink in more ways than one, rumination and worry don't necessarily happen together; they are related to different emotions and personality traits. While they both are forms of persistent negative thinking, rumination is particularly concerned with things that happened in the past—loss, sadness, disappointment, hopelessness, and failure—while worry is more focused on danger, hypothetical threats, and how to avoid them. That's probably why rumination has been linked with depression, and worry is associated with anxiety disorders (Newman, 2023).

This section is specific for ruminating-type overthinkers, people who obsess about their past, blame themselves or others, and wish they could have done things differently. If this is you, you may be spending a lot of time and energy suffering over things you can't control. Although you may think you can learn from your past, overthinking prevents you from taking action and focusing on what you can actually change about yourself or the present situation. You are dragging a useless mental load! Let's look at some actionable tips on how to let go of regret and make peace with your past:

Plan What You Can and Can't Do

We may ruminate because we believe that this way, we'll prevent bad things that have already happened to us from happening again. For example, if you break your leg by showering in the gym without flip-flops, you may spend the following two months in bed blaming yourself for "being so careless" and replaying the image of your fall over and over again.

Kimberly Drake from *PsychCentral* recommends trying to be actionable to oppose ruminations. "If you ruminate about a specific problem, sometimes inaction leads to more rumination. To rectify this, consider counteracting negative thought loops by putting those thoughts into action" (2024). Sometimes, you can learn a lesson from your past and do something about it. In this case, you may consider buying a new pair of flip-flops on Amazon and putting all your energy into your physical recovery. But there's no point in blaming yourself! Accept that some things are beyond your control, and you may have broken your leg even with your shoes on.

Other times, you can't do anything about a negative experience from your past but can work on how you look at it. For example, you went through a devastating break-up. If you keep thinking about how this person was the love of your life and you lost them, you'll have a hard time recovering! What if you start telling yourself they weren't truly that great and you know you can do better?

Come Up With New Goals

Imagine you were given the opportunity to get a scholarship and spend a year studying abroad. You made all these exciting plans for how your life would be. Sadly, the scholarship you were promised ended up going to someone else. We may ruminate because we had built a huge goal that didn't come true. We grieve the lost opportunity and the hypothetical life we had imagined.

This is where coming up with new goals helps us stop ruminating. So, you stayed at home at your usual job and with your usual friends... How about planning something exciting within your current possibilities? Maybe saving for a trip or taking an interesting class? As you connect with your present and find new opportunities ahead, you won't think as much about the possibility you left behind.

Break Your Ruminating Thoughts Into Small Parts

Do you often get tangled in complicated plots you tell yourself about the past? For example, you keep ruminating about how no one in your family understood you. Is it really so? Instead of tackling one huge element of your rumination ("my family"), break your rumination into small, more manageable parts and address each one.

Think about your mom, for instance: Can you remember a single time when she was supportive or understanding? How about your sister? What about your grandfather? You may discover that not only are you ruminating but also overgeneralizing. In any case, by breaking the thought into smaller pieces, you can disrupt your rumination and feel more in control of your thoughts.

Recognize Your Triggers

Every time you discover yourself ruminating, notice the situation you're in, including your location, the time of the day, if there's anyone with you, what you're doing, or any other triggers that have initiated the unwanted thoughts. For example, if you often have ruminations about your parents, holidays can be challenging, whether you spend them at home or not.

As you become aware of the triggers, this can help you develop strategies to prevent your rumination tendencies (Cirino, 2024).

Use Some Positive Rumination

If you are going to spend time and energy thinking about the past, you can use the positive rumination strategy, which is about intentionally thinking about positive emotions and events for a change. "The idea is that instead of spending a lot of time in negative ruminations, you can learn to ruminate about more productive things that generate positive emotions" (Bartel, 2024). The more you apply this approach, the easier it will become to spot occasions where you feel happy and turn to thoughts to trigger a positive mood. Here's what you can do:

- **Recreate a positive past event and relive all its enjoyable sensory features:** Christmas can be tricky without your grandma, yes. Can you remember how delicious her ginger cookies tasted as they crumbled in your mouth? What about when she dressed as Santa Claus, but the fake beard got tangled in an oven glove and gave her away?

- **Notice pleasant sensations in the present:** This has a lot to do with the mindfulness approach we already explained in Strategy #2. Imagine that you'll contemplate the present in the near future. Which specific details would you like to remember then, and why?

- **Replay the good talks:** Instead of ruminating about things you wish you hadn't said, choose a recent positive conversation with someone you care about. Focus on mentally replaying the nice things you both said to each other and how you felt during this special time.

Don't Worry, Be Happy!

Some overthinkers have no problem putting their past behind them, but they still miss out on the present because their mind is too busy creating dreadful futures for them. Like Martha in the story at the beginning of the chapter, worrying too much about things that are yet to happen (and most of them will never occur!) is also carrying a heavy and useless mental load you need to declutter.

This section is for readers who spend too much time creating worst-case scenarios and worrying about things beyond their control or who are concerned about possible future outcomes of their decisions. Let's explore some tips on how to stop catastrophizing and worrying about things beyond your control in the future:

Accept That Bad Things Happen Sometimes

Some overthinkers worry excessively because, deep down, they fantasize about preventing a negative outcome by visualizing it ahead. Of course, there's no such thing when the circumstances are beyond your control. While you may lower your chances of getting an illness by eating healthy and having regular check-ups, you can't prevent a thunderstorm, a train wreck, or the death of a loved one in a car crash.

At the same time, they are all unlikely to happen, so why worry "just because"? Simply tell yourself that bad things happen occasionally, but they are most likely not to happen at all. "Some things are beyond your influence, and that's okay. Focus on actions you can take, and try to let go of the rest. It's all about understanding where to channel your energy best" (Mosunic, n.d.a).

Conversely, some overthinkers tend to believe their day, week, month, or year displays a pattern and, therefore, get obsessed when something bad happens because they believe it will set the path for a future catastrophe. Again, there is no necessary correlation between everything that happens one day and the future. "Life is full of challenges as well as good and bad days. Having one bad day does not mean all days will be bad" (Nall, 2023).

Use a "Stop" Word

Therapist Alyssa Mancao recommends you get used to catching yourself in the act of catastrophizing. "Instead of viewing the [catastrophic] thought as a prediction of the future, you can simply say, 'This is a catastrophic thought. I've had these thoughts before, and things have turned out fine.'" (Volpe, 2024).

As you spot that thought in your head, it may help you to say out loud (or in your head if you are in a public place) the words "Stop," "No more," or visualize a big stop sign.

Practice Self-Care

Go back to the strategies we already explored, especially #1 and #2. Worriers need to emphasize the importance of self-care practices because catastrophic thoughts usually occur whenever we experience stress or fatigue. "Getting enough rest and engaging in stress-relieving techniques, such as exercise, meditation, and journaling, can all help a person feel better" (Nall, 2023).

Consider it a pause from your worries. Get some healthy snacks, go outside, and take a nice, long walk in nature. This may give your mind the break it was craving for!

Write Down Your Worries

Just like saying them out loud may help you see how some catastrophic thoughts sound ridiculous and make it easier to dismiss them, another helpful strategy is journaling about your worries and fears. "Confronting your anxious thoughts in this way may feel intimidating, but putting your worries on paper can allow you to break the worry cycle and leave them behind when you're done writing" (Mendez-Maldonado, 2023).

And since you spend so much time and energy visualizing future events, date them when you write them down, if possible. This will help you realize how many of them turn up not to happen at all, how many may happen but not as bad as you pictured them, and for those that eventually occur, you may find it easier to come up with a plan of action.

Limit Your Exposure to Stressors

Recognizing your triggers is a great way to keep your worry under control. That's why journaling about your overthinking is a great tool, as you may start recognizing certain patterns. Is it possible that every time you talk to your hypochondriac mother, you start worrying about your health? How about that particularly negative colleague at work? Or watching the news right before bedtime?

In any case, approach your triggers with a proactive strategy to avoid or amend them. In your mom's case, you can establish certain boundaries, such as telling her how much you care for her well-being, but you'd prefer she just share the facts with you after seeing a doctor and not discussing every little health concern with you. When it comes to information overload, you should limit your access to them and pick the right times. Although you want to remain informed of what's happening in the world, there's no reason to start worrying about a terrible event right before going to sleep.

Speaking of news, our exposure to stressors has skyrocketed in a time of social media and 24-7 connection. Setting the rule of no electronic devices an hour before bedtime or even blocking certain contacts who only share terrible stories may help you relieve some stress and cut down excessive worrying. We'll see more about limiting online content in Strategy #6.

Share Your Thoughts With Others

Sometimes, your worries become too much of a burden to carry on your own. They can weigh you down mentally and emotionally. Relying on a support system can work. "Talking to someone you trust—a friend, family member, or therapist can provide clarity. They can even help you find solutions to your worries or give you action steps toward a less stressful reality" (Mosunic, n.d.a).

I used to worry a lot when I was younger. Once, my youngest cousin, who was just 13 then, started talking to me about her fear of news of an asteroid colliding on Earth (she didn't know, but it was also one of my sources of worry).

Being the older one, I felt the responsibility to comfort her upon my shoulders, so I told her how rare the possibility of something like that happening, and besides, that it was something that totally escaped our control, so it was better to embrace life one day at a time and enjoy it. I found it surprisingly helpful!

As I stated those reassuring words out loud, it was like I was talking to myself and calming down my fears. Because of that, I strongly advise you not only to share your thoughts and ask for reassurance but also to try and reach out to people *you* can help.

More Ideas for Decluttering Your Mind

Some strategies work both for addressing ruminating and worrying tendencies. Here are some other quick, easy fixes you can put into practice whenever you spot yourself overthinking:

- **Say the thought aloud in a funny voice:** Your thoughts always seem real when they're in your head, but sometimes, they don't seem as valid when we pretend we are sharing them with someone else. "Research has shown that saying the thoughts out loud can make them seem a lot less serious and overwhelming" (Bartel, 2024). Even better, using a humorous tone can remove most of their power.

- **Try the overthinking workout:** Committing yourself to push-ups or sit-ups when you catch yourself overthinking is a great way of distracting you from your ruminations or worry—and doing some physical activity! Besides, if you hate this kind of exercise, you'll slowly educate your brain to avoid overthinking altogether.

- **Set a worry-timer:** Instead of forcing yourself to stop the rumination, grab your phone or a kitchen timer and set the alarm for five to ten minutes, giving yourself that time to ruminate. This strategy works because it reminds us that overthinking isn't outside our control but a choice we can choose not to engage in (Bartel, 2024).

In the end, the key behind these small strategies, coming from an expert like Dr. Michael Stein, is not taking your mind too seriously and not worshiping it. "Don't believe everything it says.

Don't treat your mind as a trustworthy source of information, especially about the things that make you anxious" (2019).

Key Takeaways

Rumination and worry deprive us of living in the present and potentially cause us to miss out on unique moments of our lives. Both our past and our future escape our control, so excessive thoughts constitute a heavy mental load that only drags us down. Fortunately, there are many strategies that allow us to regain control of our minds.

We can't control our thoughts, but we can get our emotions under control. That's why it's better to recognize and learn how to manage them—hence, the next chapter.

Strategy #5:

Emotional Management

The idea that you have to be protected from any kind of uncomfortable emotion is what I absolutely do not subscribe to. —John Cleese

Picture this situation: Lena's girlfriend broke up with her not so long ago. This Saturday, Lena goes to a bar with her best pal Tom and some other friends and sees her ex flirting with the bartender. Suddenly, she experiences a torrent of emotions: jealousy, rage, and sadness, all together. What does she do? She considers three possibilities:

1. Make a scene in the bar and tell her ex how she ruined her life.

2. Tell Tom she's not feeling well and go back home.

3. Look away, share with Tom how she is feeling, and then focus on having fun with her friends.

If she chooses 1, she may initially feel relieved for bursting out, but she's likely to be ashamed later and keep engaging in negative self-talk. If she chooses 2, she may find herself unable to sleep, ruminating about all the things she would like to have said to her ex. Choosing 3, on the other hand, allows her to accept she didn't like seeing her ex with another, but not giving it too much importance and not allowing this episode to ruin her night with friends. Any of us can be Lena and experience all kinds of emotions over something we can't control. However, acting out our feelings isn't always the best choice, and neither is repressing them. "Emotions that you're largely unaware of and haven't effectively addressed are liable to make themselves known in other ways, which can lead to emotional outbursts or even mental or physical illness" (Brant, 2024). There is a correlation between overthinking and emotional dysregulation. "When someone is experiencing emotional dysregulation, they may have angry outbursts, anxiety, depression, substance abuse, suicidal thoughts, self-harm, and other self-damaging behaviors" (Bhandari, 2023). And since overthinking can arise as a symptom of emotional dysregulation, understanding, expressing, and managing your emotions will help you keep your thoughts under control. This is what we'll approach in this strategy.

The Importance of Emotional Awareness

Emotions—every single one of them!—are a normal part of the human experience. We all feel angry, scared, overwhelmed, frustrated, or disappointed sometimes! Therefore, there aren't positive or negative emotions. However, what may harm us is not being able to recognize or manage them adequately. This is known as emotional dysregulation (or, colloquially, mood swings).

The first step to managing your emotions is increasing your emotional intelligence by learning to recognize, understand, and manage how you feel. Gaining emotional awareness offers many advantages, such as improving your communication skills and relationships, building intimacy, and preventing emotional outbursts and even physical illness (Brant, 2024). Here are some tips on how to do it:

- **Observe how your body feels:** If you have trouble recognizing your emotions, the first thing you should learn is to tune into your body. Pay attention to your physical sensations and notice how they correlate with specific feelings, "Take note of your posture and facial expression. Are you hunched over, trying to make yourself smaller? Are you smiling? What are your hands doing?" (*Recognizing Overthinking*, 2022). Seemingly minor changes in your body may hint at some particular emotions.

- **Journal:** Writing about how you feel over a few weeks may help you recognize your emotions and the situations or people that trigger them. "Try to label your emotions as they arise, note how your body feels in that moment, and look out for any patterns. Over time, you may be able to understand more about yourself and how you react to different things" (Brant, 2024).

- **Own your emotions:** While it may be tempting to blame others for "making you feel" a certain way, start accepting that the only person responsible for your emotions is you, "and once you start accepting responsibility for how you feel and how you behave it will have a positive impact on all areas of your life" (Roche Martin, 2022).

- **Acknowledge your triggers:** Despite being responsible for your emotions, you can monitor events, people, and circumstances that trigger them and thus limit your exposure or come up with a plan. "Practice naming and accepting the feelings—naming the feeling puts you in control. Try to choose an appropriate reaction to the feeling rather than just reacting to it" (Roche Martin, 2022).

- **Retell your story in the third person:** Do you usually mask an uncomfortable emotion with another? For example, it may be easier to feel angry than to accept that you are sad. To break this habit, try to tell yourself how you feel, but as if you were talking about someone else, describing their actions and feelings. "Jenny yells at her toddler when he spills the milk, but she's not mad at him; she's mad at herself for not paying enough attention to the child."

Deep Breathing for Emotional Regulation

When you are relaxed, you breathe at a slower pace, and when you are nervous, you breathe faster. Given the connection between breath and emotions, is it possible to manage our feelings through our breath? Yes, it is!

Breathwork, which was already mentioned when we discussed mindfulness and meditation in Strategy #2, is also an excellent tool for managing how we feel.

This is because the part of the brain that controls breath increases its pace when we experience stress. Conversely, if we voluntarily slow down our breath, we are signaling to the brain that things are okay, and it can finally relax.

"Just as speeding up your breath makes you feel more anxious and alert, though, slowing it down can make you feel calmer and more focused on the present moment" (Cooks-Campbell, 2021).

In other words, as yoga practitioners have known for millennia, controlling your breath can help you cope with negative emotions and calm your mind.

Here are some everyday examples of how to apply breathing techniques to avoid reacting to negative emotions and prevent undesired consequences:

Observe Breath to Gain Awareness

You can gain emotional awareness by simply taking a short pause to monitor your breath. Stop for a moment to observe your breath without judging it. Don't try to change its current rhythm; simply notice whatever you observe.

Imagine you notice that you are taking short breaths or are not fully expanding your abdomen as you breathe in. Start by asking yourself if any physical activity may have caused this.

Okay, so you had to climb the stairs in a hurry, good. It's your body recovering from the effort.

But what if you were reading your emails and now you're agitated? Is it possible that a message from a complaining client may have disturbed you? By observing your breath, you can perceive your current emotions instead of letting them remain hidden—possibly disturbing you for hours without realizing why.

Paced Breathing

This is a simple way to stimulate the vagus nerve, a connection between your brain and your body, and help bring physical and mental relaxation (Vogel, 2022). The objective is to spend more time exhaling than inhaling. This is how you do it:

1. Always start by noticing your current breath.

2. Inhale while mentally counting to four.

3. Hold your breath, again counting to four.

4. Exhale while counting to six.

While it may be a bit challenging at first, it will get easier as you practice it a few times. Notice how your agitation decreases as you control the rhythm of your breath.

The Breath Focus Technique

Here's a deep breathing technique that combines focus words or phrases and imagery (Cronkleton, 2024). Your focus can be anything that helps you feel more relaxed, smile, or remain neutral by distracting you from disturbing thoughts. Some examples are words like "relax," "peace," or "let go."

Here's how you do it:

1. Lie down or sit comfortably somewhere undisturbed.

2. Notice your current breath. Don't try to change it.

3. Now, alternate between your normal breaths and deep breaths a couple of times. See how your abdomen starts to expand as you inhale in deep breaths.

4. Compare your deep breaths with regular shallow breaths.

5. Practice deep breaths for a couple of minutes, with one hand placed on your stomach.

6. Combine this deep breathing with your focus of choice. Mentally say the word every time you inhale.

7. Imagine the air you inhale brings peace and calm throughout every body part.

8. Imagine the air you exhale gets rid of the accumulated tension. You can mentally say something like "let go" every time you exhale.

Bhramari, or the Humming Bee Breath

This is a yoga breathing practice you can implement to boost an instant calming sensation, relieving strong emotions such as anxiety, frustration, or anger.

Use it if you are feeling irritated to reduce your heart rate, soothe your mind, and think more clearly (Cronkleton, 2024). To practice it, go somewhere calm, if possible alone, so you can make the humming sound.

Then, follow these steps:

1. Sit comfortably and close your eyes.

2. Relax the muscles of your face.

3. Put your index fingers on each cartilage that covers your ear canal. Inhale.

4. As you exhale, gently press the fingers.

5. Make a loud humming sound with your mouth closed.

6. Keep doing this for as long as you desire.

"The more you practice your breathing, the more you will start to notice when you are under or over-breathing and identify how that contributes to your emotions," explains psychologist Alice Thornewill (Vogel, 2022).

The best part is, once you get used to breathwork, you can put it into practice anywhere and at any time—while riding public transport, waiting at a red traffic light, or even during a meeting with your team.

The Value of Stories for Understanding Your Emotions

Many of us grew up listening to fairy tales of brave heroes who saved entire villages, scary witches who could transform themselves to deceive naive children, or fierce monsters attacking innocent people. These stories serve a significant purpose in providing children with valuable emotional skills. As two famous British authors put it—first Chesterton, and then Neil Gaiman paraphrased him: "Fairy tales are more than true: not because they tell us that dragons exist, but because they tell us that dragons can be beaten" (Gaiman, 2002).

However, children aren't the only ones who benefit from stories. Research indicates that a narrative is also an effective tool for emotional regulation in adults (Pasupathi et al., 2017). Sharing your story with others helps you cope with emotions such as sadness or anger and brings new light into the events of your narrative. That's why going to a therapist is helpful for some people, but also opening up with friends they trust.

But what if you don't find the story to tell? What if you still need to work on acknowledging and managing your emotions? The right books, movies, or TV shows can help you understand and cope with your feelings, even as an adult. Reading a novel about a character coming of age may help you relate and understand the struggles you went through at that time. Exploring the relationships between fictional characters in a sitcom can provide insight into how you relate to people around you in specific contexts.

Movies, in particular, are known to significantly affect viewers. The combination of powerful music, the right script, great acting, and precise lighting and editing turn certain movies into memorable emotional lessons. "While we may view films with a varied purpose, oftentimes it's through the film that we collectively feel a similar emotion" (Bundela, 2023). Movies such as Disney-Pixar's *Up* (2009), *Inside Out* (2015), *Coco* (2017), and *Encanto* (2021), although addressed to children, offer excellent opportunities to recognize and name emotions such as regret, guilt, anger, forgiveness, compassion, and resilience.

Other movies aimed at a mature audience allow us to get in touch with profound emotions. Some recommended movies you can watch to get in touch with your deepest feelings are the sci-fi/romantic drama *Eternal Sunshine of the Spotless Mind* (2004); the biographical drama The *Pursuit of Happyness* (2006), starring Will Smith in an unforgettable role; the also awarded *Birdman* (2014) with an outstanding performance of Michael Keaton as an actor after the peak of his fame; or Barry Jenkin's Academy Award-winning *Moonlight* (2016), that deals with difficult topics such as homosexuality and Black identity.

These are only a few examples of how cinema can strongly impact viewers and even help you process emotions. "Movies are full of opportunities to learn to recognize the feelings of their different characters, to empathize, and to see how the emotions of others influence our own" (*8 Films to Develop*, 2021). By watching how these characters explore, understand, and learn to manage their emotions, you can get some valuable resources to do the same.

Practicing Empathy

Emotional intelligence is about understanding and managing your emotions, as well as understanding how others feel, identifying their emotions, and, if possible, providing them with loving support.

Developing your empathy skills is essential to strengthening your relationships. Additionally, it can help you control your overthinking. Putting yourself in the other person's shoes can prevent rumination, regret, or being overly critical. When you stop to consider how another person feels, you step out of yourself and, therefore, out of your head and its intricate web of thoughts.

Something to take into account when you are an overthinker is that empathy isn't the same as mind-reading. "Empathy is about feeling with people, not just feeling for them. When you're empathetic, you're not just guessing how someone feels. You're right there with them, feeling it too" (Mosunic, n.d.b).

Empathy offers plenty of benefits to you and others, such as developing more honest and open communication, encouraging connection, making you and the other person feel better, and building overall better relationships (marriages, parenting, friendships, and also at work).

Here are a few practical strategies for developing empathy:

- **Move out of your comfort zone:** Stick to the resolution of living new experiences and meeting new people with different backgrounds (religious, political, or ethnic) or following them on social media with an open mind. Go to see new places and cultivate your curiosity. Put yourself in a position where you have to ask for help to do something new. "Accept how helpless you may feel at times, and let it humble you. Humility can be a useful path to empathy" (Sutton, 2020).

- **Get feedback:** Get used to asking people you talk to whether they feel understood and supported. Ask them what you could do to make them feel this way. "Talk to others about what it is like to walk in their shoes—

about their issues and concerns and how they perceived experiences you both shared" (Sobel, 2016).

- **Ask better questions:** Examine your biases, which usually interfere with your listening and empathy skills. Tell yourself you can learn from anyone by just listening to what they have to say and asking them interesting questions instead of making assumptions. "When you ask thoughtful questions, you are demonstrating that you care and are curious about understanding the other person's experiences and point of view, not only different from yours but otherwise unique" (Mosunic, n.d.b).

- **Practice active listening:** When someone is talking, listen to them with your full attention, avoid distractions, and listen to understand, which means focusing on what they say instead of thinking about how to respond. Pay attention to nonverbal cues, too, such as the way they stand or their gestures.

Key Takeaways

There is a strong correlation between overthinking and emotional dysregulation. Acquiring emotional awareness and developing emotional intelligence can help you control your overthinking tendencies while improving your relationships.

- Breathwork is an excellent tool for insight and managing certain emotions.

- Narratives are powerful tools for recognizing and understanding how we feel. Movies are a particularly touching way to experience different stories.

- Developing empathy skills offers advantages for you and others, and it may prevent rumination, regret, or overly critical thinking.

We don't control our emotions, but we can—and should—be aware of what may trigger them. In today's world, being exposed to all kinds of online content can negatively affect your emotions and worsen your overthinking tendencies, and that's what the following chapter is about.

Strategy #6:

The Digital Detox

There's a danger in the internet and social media. The notion that information is enough, that more and more information is enough, that you don't have to think, you just have to get more information—gets very dangerous. –Edward de Bono

Maureen is a single mom who works as a freelancer from home.

This is what a typical weekday looks like for her:

- She wakes up with the alarm on her phone. As soon as she opens her eyes, she sees the notifications (42 unread messages, the weather, and some disturbing news about unemployment in her state and the advances of war in Europe).

- She goes to the kitchen and begins answering a few work emails from her phone while she prepares coffee. In the meantime, her children are getting ready for school.

- She sees a reminder from the group of kindergarten parents that the children are supposed to bring paper bags today, so she hurries to grab some before the school bus arrives.

- After her children leave, she gets ready to work by taking a warm shower while listening to her favorite podcast.

- She sits by her desk and goes through her list of to-do's: There's a video call scheduled for later, her online French course, and, in the afternoon, tutoring for her eldest daughter.

- At midday, during her lunch break (a few spring rolls and kung pao chicken she ordered with an app), she scrolls down on social media and checks on her friends by text messages.

- ...and so on.

We can probably relate to Maureen's routine. According to research, the average adult in the US spends 11 daily hours interacting with media (Cherry, 2023b).

Over any given day, we depend on online content in many different ways, up to the point we can't imagine our lives without our smartphones.

Through them, we communicate with other people, work, get news, entertain ourselves, study, and shop. However, heavy smartphone usage has negative aspects, and information overload is only one of them.

Being an overthinker, you must reconsider your interactions with technology. Although a complete digital detox may not be possible—or even desirable—adopting healthy habits regarding how much time we spend online (and the kind of content we access) is an essential part of coping with our overthinking tendencies and preventing stress from escalating.

In this chapter, we'll see the right strategy for being social media smart and promoting mental health and better habits.

The Consequences of Spending Too Much Time Online

We depend on our devices so much that some experts consider our immersion in the digital world a behavioral addiction (Cherry, 2023b) and, in any case, a source of stress, especially for teenagers and young adults. Emails, texts, notifications, likes, and other social media updates are constantly bombarding us. They can make us feel overwhelmed and worsen existing mental health issues. New technologies are addictive by nature, and this can lead to dependency and compulsive behavior—including, you've guessed it, overthinking.

Although there's no point in denying the importance mobile devices have in our everyday lives for working and socializing, it's worth noticing that too much time online not only distract us but also has some serious consequences for our physical and mental health, including:

- **Exposure to constant negative news:** Through social media, news sites, and even your family WhatsApp group, you are constantly receiving pieces of information that are worrying, depressing, sad, or scary—not to mention beyond your control! Positive news hardly makes it to the headlines, so basically, any news is bad news—not that it necessarily affects you directly, but it may cause anxiety and raise your stress levels. Besides, most news doesn't affect us directly. What purpose does it serve for Maureen to read about the war in Europe first thing in the morning?

- **Dopamine addiction:** Dopamine is a "feel-good" hormone released by our bodies whenever we do something pleasurable. Although it's not a substance we can get addicted to, we can develop an addiction to any activity that boosts our dopamine levels, such as eating junk food, gambling, using recreational drugs, drinking coffee, or having sex (Resnick, 2023). Social media becomes addictive because we get that "rush" whenever we scroll, get a notification, or receive likes for our posts.

- **Fear of missing out (FOMO):** Social media and hyperconnectivity make us believe that everyone is living fantastic experiences but ourselves. "You might find yourself overcommitting to social events out of the fear that you'll be left behind" (Cherry, 2023b). It also makes you reach for your phone automatically every minute.

- **Shorter attention spans:** The huge amount of stimuli we get from our screens has decreased our ability to focus on a single task for long. "Using our cell phone can become an automatic reflex and often serves no purpose. Taking a break can help us be more intentional with our time, allowing us to focus on what's more important in the moment" (*Digital Detox*, 2022).

- **Poor family life/less productivity:** You spend half the dinner listening to audio from your manager instead of being with your kids. You become distracted at work when you see notifications popping up with pictures from your daughter's ballet class. Being connected all the time may cause you not to be here or there and makes it difficult to achieve a healthy work-life balance.

- **Less time spent outdoors or exercising:** We all enjoy a good TV show or playing online video games, but an excess of these sedentary activities has the consequence of limiting our time in nature and doing much-needed physical activity.

- **Social isolation:** While we may receive several stickers or fun memes a day from our friends, when was the last time we got together for a nice talk? We may feel isolated, although we are permanently connected. Social media may also push you to constant comparison and make you feel miserable.

- **Poor sleep quality:** Device usage, especially at night, disrupts sleep. We may push our bedtime to an hour later and have trouble falling asleep. The negative effects of lack of sleep on our physical and mental health cannot be stressed enough.

But Can We Completely Unplug?

With all those negative consequences excessive device usage has for our well-being, we may wonder whether it would be better to simply shut everything off. Other than better, is it even possible? "We pay with our phones at stores, work on our computers and tablets, and maintain relationships through apps. And since the pandemic, our life-tech connection has intensified even further," explains Sophia Epstein, a BBC correspondent, who describes our modern lives as impossible to detangle from technology (2023).

It's true. We live in a world that's also digital, and there's no turning back: Our economies, our friendships, how we relate, how we communicate, how we travel or eat... everything in our modern world has been reshaped to adapt to this reality. So, no, a complete digital detox isn't possible—at least for most people.

Salesforce CEO Marc Benioff took 10 days off in an exclusive French Polynesian resort (Epstein, 2023), but I don't know many who could afford to travel to a 100% tech-free retirement in the middle of the jungle and stay disconnected for several days, do you?

Even more: For some people, the pressure of going through a full digital detox can create more stress. "As people's lives and screens are more inextricable than ever, the idealization of disconnection may end up causing more anxiety when you can't achieve it" (Epstein, 2023). Imagine not being able to pay for the check with your phone for a week or losing touch with your parents who live in another state!

Without the choice of a complete disconnection, what's left for us? Hopefully, we can attempt a partial disconnection, meaning we can be conscious about the time we spend online and choose wisely to minimize the negative effects strong device usage has on us. Next, we'll explore some alternatives to the unrealistic and almost impossible "cold turkey" approach.

Setting Realistic Goals

Knowing you can't attempt a complete disconnection, you can reduce your time online. Begin by monitoring your activity. You can install a free app to check how many times you use your phone a day and how much time you spend on social media. Afterward, set the goal of reducing your activity by a significant fraction—for example, if you discover you spend over four hours online, try to cut this time down to three.

If you set an unrealistic goal, such as just half an hour a day, you are more likely to give up when you perceive your efforts are in vain.

Taking Breaks From Social Media

Uninstalling all your social media apps and deciding you'll no longer be on Facebook or Instagram may cause you to feel socially isolated and experience FOMO. However, evidence points to several benefits when people take breaks from internet usage, especially social media. The research found lower levels of anxiety, depression, and overall well-being (Timperley, 2023). Without being too drastic, you can consider taking some breaks. For example, you may tell your contacts that you'll be disconnected during the weekend and stick to it. Spending more time outdoors or engaging in non-online activities you enjoy will help you maintain your goal—as well as knowing your loved ones can still reach you through your phone if there's an emergency.

Not posting any stories or content on your Instagram feed won't kill you, and you don't need to catch up on every single one of your acquaintances. On the contrary, taking a break from social media, although it isn't the same as fully disconnecting yourself, may have a positive effect on your mental health. Try it for a day, and then see if you can make this weekend breaks a regular habit.

Being Proactive in Device Usage

According to Sina Joneidy, a senior lecturer in digital enterprise at Teesside University, UK, while we can't shut down technology, we can attempt to detox from our desirous attachment to it—meaning, stop considering it something that makes us happy—and practice digital mindfulness, which may be a more practical approach: "less worry about cutting tech out entirely, and more focus on being intentional with its use" (Epstein, 2023). This means no longer reaching for your phone during every break to scroll down social media and using devices only intentionally. Answering a text message from your mom is a yes, but checking notifications every hour is a no.

Here are some tips you can apply right away to limit your device usage proactively:

- Unsubscribe from mail lists you hardly read.

- Unfollow accounts that stress you.

- Uninstall games and apps you are spending too much time with—later, you can reinstall them, but sometimes you'll notice you're just as good without them!

- Reduce your contact list.

- Deactivate notifications from all your apps.

- Set a black-and-white background screen—even better, the whole phone configuration!

Tips for Making the Best Out of Your Internet Use

If you find yourself constantly reaching for your phone and you find it stressful whenever you can't find it, here are some small, actionable steps to reduce (although not completely shut down) your screentime:

- **Set device-free places in the house:** Start by leaving your phone out of specific rooms of your house. For example, you can't bring it to your baby's nursery or to your bedroom.

- **Schedule daily breaks:** Instead of attempting a full disconnection on the weekend, start by designating technology-free times, such as during meals, when you work out, or before finishing your breakfast. This will allow you to fully enjoy these moments with the people you love or by yourself.

- **Turn off the phone before bedtime:** Build the habit of putting away your phone 30 minutes to an hour before going to sleep. "Smartphones were designed to keep us alert and productive, so the last thing we want is to bombard our brains with more information" (Addarich Martinez, 2024).

- **Use tech in your favor:** Just like some apps are designed to release dopamine, others help you monitor your phone usage and social media time. Use them to gain awareness and reduce your online activity.

- **Focus on adding activities to your day:** Just like you may eat healthier when you put your mind to eating new, more nutritious meals instead of cutting off junk food, you may significantly reduce your screen time when you schedule other non-online activities you enjoy. This weekend, commit to spending more time outdoors, meeting a friend for coffee, spending time with your children, cooking a new recipe, visiting your local library, or taking a nap. The reduction of device usage follows as a consequence.

Key Takeaways

Our digital lives are an undeniable part of our real lives, so the idea of completely unplugging ourselves from technology isn't just unrealistic but may also cause us additional stress. However, with the right strategies, we can counteract some negative effects of social media and heavy device usage.

- Be aware of the adverse effects new technologies can have on you and which kind of content or interactions trigger your overthinking.

- Don't attempt a complete digital detox. Instead, practice mindful technology usage and be proactive in your online activities.

- Consider taking regular breaks from social media.

- Focus on activities you enjoy and meet your friends in person whenever you can.

This strategy (and the previous ones) doesn't provide a once-and-for-all fix for overthinking; rather, you have to incorporate healthy habits into your life. Hence, the last chapter of this book.

Strategy #7: Creating a Mind-Clearing Routine

There's no way that a clear mind can live an unhappy life. –Katie Byron

We started this journey toward mental decluttering by underlining how overthinking is not a disease to be cured or a flaw to be eradicated but a learned habit we have gotten used to. It may be useful in some specific instances in your life, but at the same time, it has many negative consequences for your overall well-being.

What's the best way to get rid of a nasty habit? Easy: Replace it with a healthier one! Instead of hitting your hand every time you reach for your phone, you can fight excessive device usage by adopting non-screen habits such as jogging outdoors, cooking, or meeting every week with your friends.

Instead of biting your nails to prevent you from lighting a cigarette, you can smoke less by practicing breathing exercises. And instead of punishing yourself every time you have fries, you can get used to ordering salads as a side dish.

As for overthinking, the previous strategies we've explored in this book work better when you don't consider them quick fixes but turn them into daily habits. This way, your overthinking tendencies may remain with you, but you can learn to keep them under control and prevent them from interfering with your life and happiness.

In this final chapter, we'll look into other ways you can embrace a healthier life for your mental well-being and overcome the adverse effects of overthinking with small, consistent actions in your daily routine. Don't try to achieve it all at once, though; it's the little steps that count!

Start Your Day With a Clear Mind

Be realistic: You won't change every single habit in a day. However, you can create a new routine to improve your quality of life and reduce your overthinking, starting with mornings. When you start your day right, you'll likely experience many benefits. Morning routines set the tone for the rest of the day, so if you manage to create good habits for the first 30 minutes, the positive effects will remain uplifting your mood and energy for much longer.

There isn't a one-size-fits-all morning routine, as much of it depends on your current habits, preferences, and lifestyle. You should design one you're comfortable with, starting with small steps. Once you get used to doing something, it will come naturally, and you can move on to adding another positive change. Here are some tips for creating a great morning routine. Again, don't try them all at once if they don't sound anything like you, but go little by little instead.

- **Get an early start:** Many successful people—for example, billionaire entrepreneur Richard Branson—mention how an early start is the key to their productivity (Monroe, 2024). Starting your routine as early as 5 or 6 a.m. can help you gain precious, uninterrupted "me" time you can invest in meditating, journaling, exercising, and planning the rest of the day with a positive mindset.

- **Avoid your phone:** It's okay to use your phone as an alarm as long as you don't feel tempted to spend your first minutes awake catching up on notifications. If this is your case, get an old alarm clock for your nightstand and leave your phone in another room.

- **Think positive thoughts:** Before getting up, spend those first few minutes after you wake up practicing positive affirmations, meditating, or praying. Tell yourself how this new day offers a new opportunity. You can also write down your thoughts or things you're grateful for.

- **Get air, water, and nutrition:** After several hours of sleep, your body needs to replenish its fluids and gain energy. Instead of hurrying to the kitchen to begin an excessive caffeine intake, get used to leaving a bottle of water beside your bed. "While dehydration leaves you feeling drained and sluggish, guzzling some water after waking up flushes toxins that have built up in your system overnight and gives your metabolism a little boost," explains Deep Patel from *Entrepreneur* (2019). Some light breathing exercises and a healthy breakfast will help you boost your energy and feel happier and ready to tackle the daily challenges.

- **Strengthen bonds:** Every morning, before you rush to work, spend some minutes connecting with your family, including your furry friends. "If you have pets, make them a part of this time," says Nicole Spector from *Better by Today* (2018), since sometimes we overlook the positive benefits of spending quality time with those we love and the business and stress of the day make it easy to neglect our bonds.

- **Listen to music:** Listening to music has plenty of positive effects, such as boosting your mood and relieving stress, improving your concentration and memory, and promoting neuroplasticity (which refers to the ability of your brain to learn) (Raypole, 2020). So, instead of turning on the TV or the radio and starting your day with depressing news, opt for fun music during your mornings. If you need to know anything, you'll find out about it on your way to work or later during the day, but there's no need to overload your mind with information just yet. Using your mind to plan your goals for the day while listening to something you enjoy is better.

The Power of Journaling

We won't dig too deep into this part of the strategy because we've already mentioned more than once the importance of journaling to free your mind and prevent overthinking from taking a toll on your mental well-being. You may remember how journaling has appeared as part of other strategies, such as gaining emotional awareness or spotting cognitive distortions. Here are some benefits of journaling as a daily habit (Sutton, 2018):

- It reduces your stress and anxiety.

- It improves your awareness and perception of events.

- It helps you regulate and cope with all kinds of emotions.

- It encourages recovery from trauma.

- It may even enhance your physical health.

No matter which overthinking type(s) you identify yourself with, creative writing helps you ease your thoughts. If you struggle with indecisiveness or perfectionism, journaling can help you achieve your goals. "When you use your journal to write down your goals, you can keep better track of your intentions. This will help you stay accountable and serve as a reminder of what you need to do to reach your goals" (Kaiser Permanente, 2020). Journaling will also boost your self-confidence, allowing you to track your progress and personal growth.

There is no single way of journaling. Some people make lists, jot down their thoughts, or explore their inner voice in other ways. Doodling and drawing are also okay! So, if you haven't bought a cute notebook and left it in a visible place, do it now. It's a cheap way to tackle overthinking and embrace better mental health.

Time Management as a Decluttering Tool

Thomas is a single dad who right now needs to focus on his work as a real estate salesman. However, he can't concentrate because he's thinking about the parent-teacher meeting he has in the afternoon, the empty fridge he needs to fill on his way home, and the leaky faucet he needs to fix because, otherwise, it will keep him up at night—again! As he drives home after a long day with clients, he finds he still can't stop thinking about all those things he should have done but didn't get to.

Can you relate? Having too many things to do clutters your mind. This is something many workers complain about: It's called the mental load. According to a 2019 study by Ifop-Mooncard, 95% of people admitted they can't stop thinking about their work during the evenings, and 77% of them state they have too many tasks to manage simultaneously (*10 Tips to Free Yourself*, 2019). This makes them feel constantly tired and unable to unwind. As we've seen in Strategy #6, permanent connectivity only increases that feeling.

Stay-at-home parents also experience a mental load, which takes the form of invisible, never-ending, exhausting work that knows no boundaries because it also involves emotional tasks when taking care of others. There's no way to predict this kind of emotional work. Plus, you must manage your own emotions and how you react to them before addressing the emotional needs of the people around you (UCLA Health, 2024).

Carrying a mental load makes you feel drained and exhausted, even without any physical effort. "A cognitive task such as remembering which groceries to buy may not seem like much. But when those invisible tasks accumulate and the load gets heavy, it can affect your relationships, physical health, and mental well-being" (UCLA Health, 2024).

On the contrary, organizing your schedule and using the right time management tools will relieve your mental load and reduce overthinking. Here are some strategies to mentally "unload" yourself and declutter your mind from those small, accumulating tasks:

Break Big Tasks Into Steps

Some chores that are necessary to keep up a home seem endless and may cause unnecessary stress if you visualize them as items in your "to-do" list. For example, "Clean the house" or "Get groceries." But let's be real: Your house will rarely be 100% clean—except right after completing your spring cleaning—and there's always some item missing you may need to buy later! So, it's better to list quick, actionable steps you can tackle in the day: "Clean the toilet," "Wipe kitchen counter,"

"Make the beds," "Take out the trash," or "Buy milk, eggs, and cereals at the supermarket" seem more achievable, right?

Use Calendars, Schedules, and Lists

You may have a heavy workload, but you don't need to mentally carry it around with you! There are plenty of apps that will help you sort your priorities and keep a global vision of what needs to be accomplished while at the same time visualizing what's not as important or can be delegated. "Writing down what we must do clears the mind and, at the same time, helps us memorize the tasks. By putting words to thoughts, these tasks look less daunting, and we can organize our days more rationally" (*5 Helpful Tools*, 2022).

Maintain a Pleasant Workspace

A cluttered desk or home office won't do you any good regarding your mental load. On the other hand, an aesthetic, friendly workspace contributes to your well-being and positively affects your productivity. "At the office or your home office, even the little things matter. On your desk or in the room where you work, add some decorative elements, such as pictures of your friends or a green plant" (*10 Tips to Free Yourself*, 2019).

Look After Yourself

Recognizing your mental load is the first step. Talking about it and asking for help is the second. Set clear boundaries, and don't take on more tasks than you can manage. Discuss it with your manager to come up with a solution together. "For this discussion to be fruitful, give specific examples, quantified if possible (the number of unread emails in the queue, the time needed to complete a task, etc.)" (*10 Tips to Free Yourself*, 2019). At home, in addition to learning to say no and delegating tasks to your partner, include your children if you have them and assign them some age-appropriate responsibilities, such as packing their lunches or folding laundry.

Finally, choose how you spend your time and list pleasurable activities, no matter how busy your daily schedule is. Research conducted by the University of Nebraska shows that as little as 12 minutes of laughter can boost your energy levels. "A song, dance, pillow or tickle fight can help relieve stress for you and your children" (*5 Helpful Tools*, 2022).

The Value of Social Support

Finally, to live a life free of overthinking (at least, most of the time!), it's essential to surround yourself with people you love—possibly involving them in your strategies and asking for support and help. "Acknowledging and vocalizing how you're feeling will ease your mental strain. Cooperation lends new perspectives on a problem and will lighten your load" (Perry, 2022). This doesn't mean they are responsible for your thoughts or well-being (remember, you are the single responsible one!), but educating and making them take part in some of your new habits may help you stick to them.

When I first started meditating, I found that consistency was the hardest part. I would happily meditate for five minutes one day, feel fantastic, and then forget about the whole thing for a week. However, after I talked to my partner, we decided to set the goal of daily meditating together. We pushed each other into the habit, and now we always practice some exercises before we go to bed. If you find it hard to fight worry or rumination, speaking to a friend you trust about your problems can help, both for distracting you and as a highly effective coping method, according to Elizabeth Scott from *Very Well Mind* (2023). However, you must be careful not to fall into co-rumination, which is what happens when you and your friend keep talking about the same issues over and over. "If you find yourself dwelling only on the negative when talking to a friend, it's likely that you are engaging in non-helpful co-rumination," which may look supportive but only increases your anxiety and mental fog, explains Scott.

Being with friends can help even if you don't talk about the subject of your overthinking. Maybe watching a fun movie together or making each other laugh is all you need. "Even if you choose not to discuss your problems, the simple act of getting together with a friend can be useful to clear your mind" (Scott, 2023).

Try to spend time with people who help you feel great about yourself. Finally, remember there's always the possibility of going to a therapist if you notice you can't control overthinking. Don't hesitate to ask for professional help if, after everything you've tried, you think you may need it.

Key Takeaways

As difficult as it may be, overthinking is not more than an acquired habit, and as it happens in other instances, the best way to fight it is by integrating new, healthier habits into our daily lives.

- Create a great morning routine to start your day in a positive mood that will set the tone for the following hours.

- If you haven't taken up the habit of journaling, start today, as it offers huge benefits.

- Learn time management skills to reduce your mental load.

- Rely on your friends and family; they can greatly help even if you don't share your worries with them!

At this point, remember to pat yourself on the back and congratulate yourself on your progress! The overthinking detox isn't a goal you'll reach once and for all, but a way of life—one you have already embraced, and it's beginning to show its results.

Conclusion

Congratulations on getting up to this stage of your journey! By now, you are equipped with the most effective strategies for coping with your overthinking tendencies in daily life, thus preventing all those negative consequences they may have when left unattended. You have learned that overthinking is not a disease—although it may have consequences both for your physical and mental health.

No matter your overthinking type, you can recognize it as a habit deeply embedded in you. You can nonetheless change by embracing new, healthier habits and consistently putting them into practice: taking care of your body, meditating, spotting your cognitive distortions and reshaping your beliefs, letting go of the past and the future that can't be controlled, managing your emotions, limiting your exposure to stressors (especially in the digital world), and embracing practices for keeping your mind clear from all clutter.

If you are still not applying some of the strategies explored, do it now, even if you are feeling fine—*especially* if you are feeling fine! This will make it easier for you to seize the resource in time of need.

You will still experience overthinking sometimes, but now you are empowered with all you have learned, and it won't control your life anymore. Know that managing your thoughts and emotions isn't a goal you reach once and for all but a lifetime journey. Don't feel discouraged when things get tough. We all struggle, and you can always reach out for help. Thank you for trusting me and walking along the same path toward this mind detox journey. It's been a privilege to guide you! I only ask you one last favor:

If you learned something valuable from reading this book and it helped you achieve control and understanding of your overthinking, kindly leave a review so other readers can also benefit from these seven strategies and start applying them in their lives for achieving a much-needed mind cleanse.

I wish you plenty of happy, calm, and mindful moments. You deserve them! Life is a journey, and our thoughts and memories are the only baggage that matters. Carry just the important ones and travel light!

Glossary

CBT: Cognitive behavioral therapy, a form of psychological treatment used for addressing several mental issues. Its core is addressing unhelpful thinking, learned patterns, and behavior to replace them with positive ones.

Cognitive distortion: A thought a person has that causes them to perceive reality inaccurately, mostly in negative ways.

Dopamine: The "feel-good" hormone our body produces whenever we do something pleasurable.

Emotional dysregulation: A poor emotional response, whether by failing to acknowledge what you feel or reacting in inappropriate ways to your emotions.

Endorphins: "Feel-good" hormones our bodies release when we exercise.

FOMO: Fear of missing out, or the false perception created by overexposure to social media that everyone's lives are better than ours.

Mental load: The cognitive work the mind makes to keep track of everything necessary to work, run a house, manage relationships, etc. It can leave a person exhausted and drained despite not making any physical effort.

Nutritional psychiatry: A relatively new field in medicine that studies the link between the brain and the gut.

Rumination: A specific type of overthinking that consists of obsessively thinking about past events (mostly negative ones).

Serotonin: A chemical substance in our brains that creates feelings of happiness and well-being.

References

Ackerman, C.E. (2018, February 12). *Cognitive restructuring techniques for reframing thoughts.* Positive Psychology. https://positivepsychology.com/cbt-cognitive-restructuring-cognitive-distortions/

Addarich Martinez, N. (2024, August 22). *Social media detox: How to unplug for better mental health.* Cnet. https://www.cnet.com/health/mental/social-media-detox/

American Heart Association. (2024, March 21). *Spend time in nature to reduce stress and anxiety.* https://www.heart.org/en/healthy-living/healthy-lifestyle/stress-management/spend-time-in-nature-to-reduce-stress-and-anxiety

American Psychological Association. (2017). *What is cognitive behavioral therapy?* https://www.apa.org/ptsd-guideline/patients-and-families/cognitive-behavioral

Angelou, M. (n.d.). *"If you must look back...".* [Quote]. GoodReads. https://www.goodreads.com/quotes/6849181-if-you-must-look-back-do-so-forgivingly-if-you

Bartel, J. (2024, June 6). *How to stop ruminating: 15 tips from a therapist.* Choosing Therapy. https://www.choosingtherapy.com/how-to-stop-ruminating/

Bence, S. (2024, July 19). *Grounding techniques: connecting with nature for better health.* Very Well Health. https://www.verywellhealth.com/grounding-7494652

Bhandari, S. (2023, July 19). *What is emotional dysregulation?* WebMD. https://www.webmd.com/mental-health/what-is-emotional-dysregulation

Brant, A. (2024, April 20). *Developing emotional awareness: benefits and tips.* Better Help. https://www.betterhelp.com/advice/general/developing-emotional-awareness/

Bundela, R. (2023, February 12). *9 movies to help you process your emotions.* Movieweb. https://movieweb.com/movies-to-help-process-your-emotions/

Byron, K. (n.d.). *"There's no way that a clear mind...".* [Quote]. AZ Quotes. https://www.azquotes.com/quote/873216?ref=clear-minds

Camacho, B. (2024, February 28). *Why do I overthink everything?* Talkatry. https://www.talkiatry.com/blog/why-do-i-overthink-everything

Carver, C. (2012). *Digital Detox: how to unplug for the weekend.* Be More With Less. https://bemorewithless.com/digitaldetox/

Cherry, K. (2023a, November 2). *What Is Cognitive Behavioral Therapy (CBT)?* Very Well Mind. https://www.verywellmind.com/what-is-cognitive-behavior-therapy-2795747

Cherry, K. (2023b, October 31). *How to do a digital detox.* Very Well Mind. https://www.verywellmind.com/why-and-how-to-do-a-digital-detox-4771321

Chrichton-Stuart, C. & Dias, A. (2024, January 16). *What are some foods to ease anxiety?* Medical News Today. https://www.medicalnewstoday.com/articles/322652

Cirino, E. (2024, June 6). *12 tips to help you stop ruminating.* Healthline. https://www.healthline.com/health/how-to-stop-ruminating

Cleese, J. (n.d.). *"The idea that you have to be protected...".* [Quote]. GoodReads. https://www.goodreads.com/quotes/7486997-the-idea-that-you-have-to-be-protected-from-any

Cognitive distortions: Understanding overgeneralization. (2021, January 12). Therapy Now SF. https://www.therapynowsf.com/blog/cognitive-distortions-understanding-overgeneralization

Conway, S. (2020). *How meditation helps stop overthinking.* Mindworks. https://mindworks.org/blog/how-meditation-helps-stop-overthinking/

Cooks-Campbell, A. (2021, August 19). *Breathwork: The secret to emotional regulation.* Better Up. https://www.betterup.com/blog/breathwork

Cronkleton, E. (2024, May 17). *10 breathing exercises to try when you're feeling stressed.* Healthline. https://www.healthline.com/health/breathing-exercise

De Bono, E. (n.d.). *"There is a danger in the Internet and social media..."*. [Quote]. Brainyquote. https://www.brainyquote.com/topics/social-media-quotes

Digital detox: Take a break from technology to boost mental health. (2022, February 7). Nebraska Medicine. https://www.nebraskamed.com/behavioral-health/digital-detox-take-a-break-from-technology-to-boost-mental-health

Drake, K. (2024, June 26). *9 tips to help stop ruminating.* PsychCentral. https://psychcentral.com/health/tips-to-help-stop-ruminating

8 films to develop emotional intelligence. (2021, July 15). FilmThreat. https://filmthreat.com/features/8-films-to-develop-emotional-intelligence/

Epstein, S. (2023, March 16). *Is it possible to digital detox anymore?* BBC. https://www.bbc.com/worklife/article/20230313-is-it-possible-to-digital-detox-anymore

Examples of cognitive restructuring. (n.d.). Concordia University. https://www.concordia.ca/cunews/offices/provost/health/topics/stress-management/cognitive-restructuring-examples.html

5 helpful tools to decrease your mental load. (2022). Share(d). https://share-d.com/en/blog/breathe/lighten-my-mental-load/5-tools-to-decrease-mental-load/

Ford, H. (n.d.). *"Whether you think you can..."*. [Quote]. GoodReads. https://www.goodreads.com/quotes/978-

whether-you-think-you-can-or-you-think-you-can-t--
you-re

Gaiman, N. (2022). *Coraline*. Avon Books.

Grinspoon, P. (2022, May 4). *How to recognize and tame your cognitive distortions*. Harvard Health Publishing. https://www.health.harvard.edu/blog/how-to-recognize-and-tame-your-cognitive-distortions-202205042738

Gupta, A. (2022, April 29). *Are you stuck in the vicious cycle of overthinking? It's risky, warns an expert*. Health Shots. https://www.healthshots.com/mind/mental-health/heres-how-overthinking-can-impact-your-overall-health/

Hartney, E. (2023, November 8). *10 cognitive distortions that can cause negative thinking*. Very Well Mind. https://www.verywellmind.com/ten-cognitive-distortions-identified-in-cbt-22412

Hoshaw, C. (2022, March 29). *What is mindfulness? A simple practice for greater well-being*. Healthline. https://www.healthline.com/health/mind-body/what-is-mindfulness

How do smartphones affect mental health? (2023). Therapy Brands. https://therapybrands.com/blog/what-is-the-impact-of-smartphone-addiction-on-mental-health/

Huffmire, A. (2023, September 28). *The life-changing morning routine to help clear your mind*. Brain MD. https://brainmd.com/blog/best-morning-routine-to-help-clear-your-mind/

Jones, H. (2023, October 2). *10 exercises that help you stop overthinking.* Very Well Health. https://www.verywellhealth.com/how-to-stop-overthinking-7570368

Kaiser Permanente. (2020, March 24). *Why everyone should keep a journal — 7 surprising benefits.* https://healthy.kaiserpermanente.org/health-wellness/healtharticle.7-benefits-of-keeping-a-journal

MasterClass. (2022, April 28). *Overthinking meaning: How to stop overthinking.* https://www.masterclass.com/articles/overthinking

Mayo Clinic. (2022, October 11). *Mindfulness exercises.* https://www.mayoclinic.org/healthy-lifestyle/consumer-health/in-depth/mindfulness-exercises/art-20046356

McGregor, P. (2018, December 3). *Using mindfulness to stop overthinking.* Paul McGregor. http://www.pmcgregor.com/mindfulness-stop-overthinking/

Mendez-Maldonado, C. (2023, June 9). *5 tips on how to stop worrying about everything.* Talkatry. https://www.talkiatry.com/blog/how-to-stop-worrying

Mindful. (2020, July 8). *What is mindfulness?* https://www.mindful.org/what-is-mindfulness/

Mindful. (2019). *How to meditate.* https://www.mindful.org/how-to-meditate/

Monroe, J. (2024, June 24). *Morning routines: 17 ways to jump-start a more productive day.* Motion. https://www.usemotion.com/blog/morning-routines

Morin, A. (2024, June 18). *How to stop overthinking.* Very Well Mind. https://www.verywellmind.com/how-to-know-when-youre-overthinking-5077069

Mosunic, C. (n.d.a). *How to stop worrying: 8 tips to overcome an anxiety cycle.* Calm. https://www.calm.com/blog/how-to-stop-worrying

Mosunic., C. (n.d.b). *How to be more empathetic: 8 exercises to develop empathy.* Calm. https://www.calm.com/blog/how-to-be-more-empathetic

Nall, R. (2023, November 30). *How to stop catastrophizing.* Medical News Today. https://www.medicalnewstoday.com/articles/320844

Nelson, L. (2023, November 5). *Why do I overthink everything: Causes, effects, and strategies.* AFA Education. https://afaeducation.org/blog/why-do-i-overthinking-everything-causes-effects-and-strategies/

Newman, K.H. (2023, January 13). *Worry and rumination enhance a positive emotional contrast based on the framework of the Contrast Avoidance Model.* J Anxiety Disord. 2023 Mar;94:102671. doi: 10.1016/j.janxdis.2023.102671. Epub 2023 Jan 13. PMID: 36681058; PMCID: PMC10071830.

Overthinking: the 9 different types, 50+ quotes & how to stop. (2023). The Depression Project.

https://thedepressionproject.com/blogs/news/the-9-different-types-of-overthinking

Pasupathi M., Wainryb C., Mansfield C.D., Bourne S. (2017, April). The feeling of the story: Narrating to regulate anger and sadness. *Cogn Emot.* 2017 Apr;31(3):444-461. doi: 10.1080/02699931.2015.1127214. Epub 2016 Jan 8. PMID: 26745208; PMCID: PMC5584785.

Patel, D. (2019, January 14). *The 10-minute morning routine that will clear your mind.* Entrepreneur. https://www.entrepreneur.com/living/the-10-minute-morning-routine-that-will-clear-your-mind/325493

Perry, E. (2022, March 3). *Lost in a mental fog? Here are 5 ways to clear your mind.* Better Up. https://www.betterup.com/blog/how-to-clear-your-mind

Pollock, D.M. (2023, November 29). *What are cognitive distortions?* Medical News Today. https://www.medicalnewstoday.com/articles/cognitive-distortions

Ramesh, A. (2022, February 2). *Overthinking: simple ways to stop overthinking and ease anxiety symptoms.* MedIndia. https://www.medindia.net/health/lifestyle/overthinking-simple-ways-to-stop-overthinking-and-ease-anxiety-symptoms.htm

Ravikant, N. (n.d.). *"A fit body, a calm mind..."*. [Quote]. GoodReads. https://www.goodreads.com/quotes/9221707-a-fit-body-a-calm-mind-a-house-full-of

Raypole, C. (2024, January 29). *30 grounding techniques to quiet distressing thoughts.* Healthline. https://www.healthline.com/health/grounding-techniques

Raypole, C. (2020, November 11). *8 ways to give your mind a deep cleaning.* Healthline. https://www.healthline.com/health/mental-health/how-to-clean-your-mind

Recognizing overthinking and how to stop: DBT emotion regulation skills. (2022, October 20). Kind Mind Psychology. https://www.kindmindpsych.com/recognizing-overthinking-and-how-to-stop-dbt-emotion-regulation-skills/

Resnick, A. (2023, September 13). *Can you be addicted to dopamine?* Very Well Mind. https://www.verywellmind.com/can-you-get-addicted-to-dopamine-5207433

Roche Martin. (2022, January 12). *50 tips for improving your emotional intelligence.* https://www.rochemartin.com/blog/50-tips-improving-emotional-intelligence

Sawchuck, C. (2017). *Coping with anxiety: Can diet make a difference?* Mayo Clinic. https://www.mayoclinic.org/diseases-conditions/generalized-anxiety-disorder/expert-answers/coping-with-anxiety/faq-20057987

Scott, E. (2024, January 15). *5 meditation techniques to get you started.* Very Well Mind.

https://www.verywellmind.com/different-meditation-techniques-for-relaxation-3144696

Scott, E. (2023, November 28). *6 effective ways to clear your mind.* Very Well Mind. https://www.verywellmind.com/how-can-i-clear-my-mind-3144602

7 reasons to break your smartphone addiction. (n.d.). Piedmont. https://www.piedmont.org/living-real-change/does-your-smartphone-cause-anxiety

Silva Casabianca, S. (2022, January 11). *15 cognitive distortions to blame for negative thinking.* PsychCentral. https://psychcentral.com/lib/cognitive-distortions-negative-thinking

Sobel, A. (2016). *Eight ways to improve your empathy.* Andrew Sobel. https://andrewsobel.com/article/eight-ways-to-improve-your-empathy/

Soong, K. (2024, January 9). *7 brain foods that can help you beat anxiety.* The Washington Post. https://www.washingtonpost.com/wellness/2024/01/09/food-diet-reduce-anxiety/

Spector, N. (2018, September 20). *A 30-minute morning routine that will clear your mind and banish stress.* Better by Today, NBC News. https://www.nbcnews.com/better/health/30-minute-morning-routine-will-clear-your-mind-banish-stress-ncna911146

Star, K. (2023, January 3). *The mental health benefits of physical exercise.* Very Well Mind.

https://www.verywellmind.com/mental-health-benefits-of-exercise-2584094

Stein, M. (2019, August 21). *Thoughts are just thoughts: How to stop worshiping your anxious mind.* Anxiety & Depression Association of America. https://adaa.org/learn-from-us/from-the-experts/blog-posts/consumer/thoughts-are-just-thoughts

Sutton, J. (2020, September 16). *How to develop empathy: 10 exercises & worksheets.* Positive Psychology. https://positivepsychology.com/empathy-worksheets/

Sutton, J. (2018, May 14). *5 benefits of journaling for mental health.* Positive Psychology. https://positivepsychology.com/benefits-of-journaling/

10 tips to free yourself from mental load at work. (2019). Hays. https://www.hays.lu/en/blogs/tips-mental-load-work

3 ways getting outside into nature helps improve your health. (2023, May 3). Cultivating Health. https://health.ucdavis.edu/blog/cultivating-health/3-ways-getting-outside-into-nature-helps-improve-your-health/2023/05

Timperley, J. (2023, August 21). *Why going on a tech-free holiday may not be the cure for burnout.* BBC Science Focus. https://www.sciencefocus.com/comment/unplugging-holidays-well-being

Tolle, E. (2004). *The Power of Now: A Guide to Spiritual Enlightenment.* New World Library.

Tools to stop overthinking. (n.d.). Fernwood Fitness. https://www.fernwoodfitness.com.au/library/blogs/to ols-to-stop-overthinking

Toshi, N. (2024, May 6). *Overthinking—To what extent can it damage your life?* PharmEasy. https://pharmeasy.in/blog/overthinking-to-what-extent-can-it-damage-your-life/

UCLA Health. (2024, January 8). *Mental load: What it is and how to manage it.* https://www.uclahealth.org/news/article/mental-load-what-it-and-how-manage-it

Vilhauer, J. (2020, September 27). *How your thinking creates your reality.* Psychology Today. https://www.psychologytoday.com/intl/blog/living-forward/202009/how-your-thinking-creates-your-reality

Vogel, K. (2022, March 3). *Breathing rhythms can affect your emotions: here's how.* PsychCentral. https://psychcentral.com/lib/change-how-you-feel-change-how-you-breathe

Volpe, A. (2024, February 3). *Are you catastrophizing? Here's how to stop assuming the worst.* Vox. https://www.vox.com/even-better/24055564/catastrophizing-stop-assuming-the-worst-negative-thoughts

Watts, A. (2022). *Allan Watts: Don't think too much.* Teach Thought. https://www.teachthought.com/critical-thinking/alan-watts-dont-think-too-much/

What causes overthinking and how to overcome It? (2022). Refocus. https://refocus.com.au/what-causes-overthinking-and-how-to-overcome-it/

Wilding, M. (2024, February 7). *3 types of overthinking — and how to overcome them.* Harvard Business Review. https://hbr.org/2024/02/3-types-of-overthinking-and-how-to-overcome-them

Witmer, S.A. (2023, March 24). *What is overthinking, and how do I stop overthinking everything?* GoodRx Health. https://www.goodrx.com/health-topic/mental-health/how-can-i-stop-overthinking-everything

Youngblood Gregory, S. (2024, March 4). *The mental health benefits of nature: Spending time outdoors to refresh your mind.* Mayo Clinic. https://mcpress.mayoclinic.org/mental-health/the-mental-health-benefits-of-nature-spending-time-outdoors-to-refresh-your-mind/

Made in United States
Orlando, FL
13 March 2025

59441433R10069